TURNT(L)ABLE

dj equipment | records | videos | clothing | reading material | design

turntable lab online store
http://turntablelab.com

turntable lab store front
120 e.7th st. manhattan, new york
212.677.0675

turntable lab hq (po po relocated us)
20 jay st. #1014. brooklyn, ny 11201

%50 FUK YOUR LIFE, HOP ON MY 98 DIRTBIKE...
(tony says to pete: you gonna put some shit that doesn't mean anything under the pictures?)

%100   %75   %50   %25   repetitive elements

forthcoming lab projectos: rehash 45, diplodocus lp, struggle inc collabo, taliban collabo
likes: dumbo, plywood, terps / dislikes: sillysburg, lakers, cool kids.

the lab time summer 02 coming soon.

6	THE ACADEMIC ARCHIVE
9	PRETTY PURDIE
24	BOB JAMES CALLING
27	TWO BROTHERS WITH BEATS
31	OLD SCHOOL: FIRST PHASE
36	NORTH COAST HIP-HOP
40	LOVE AND HATE: GROOVE MERCHANT
43	MUSIC MOBILITY
46	TEXAS FUNK SUNNY SIDE UP: TIMOTHY MCNEALY
52	TAPE CHECK
53	THE ELITE 20
57	IN THE BEDROOM
64	THE HUMAN ELEMENT: MALCOM CATTO
67	BONGO FLAVA
73	COMMON GROUND
78	CUTTING CORNERS
81	RE:DISCOVERY
83	CHECK YOUR BUCKET!
86	FIRE CORNER SOUNDS
92	THE MEMOIRS OF PRINCE PAUL

On December 15th 2001, Wax Poetics modestly debuted at select spots around the country. What had begun a year earlier as an idea in the World Trade Center had become reality. Last August, I was fired from the software development firm I had worked at for two years. I thought it was a blessing; I'd get to concentrate more on the magazine. It turned out to be a blessing in more ways than one. The structure that housed the thoughts that became this reality is no longer a reality itself; it exists only as a collection of memories. I decided not to waste any more time, and would pour my passion into Wax Poetics. I vowed that Wax Poetics would be the beginning of something new, a fresh perspective on the music I cared about. Unlike other magazines that treat the culture like fodder, I would create something lasting, relatively speaking. The response we've received since the debut issue hit shelves has been overwhelming. I want to thank everyone who sent letters and emails—please keep them coming. We're now available worldwide, and our distribution network is growing by the day. Subscription service will soon be available as well, for those who have asked, so check our website for information. As happy as we are with the first issue, it was a mere primer, a glimmer of our full potential. With this issue, we expand our reach and dig a little deeper. This has been a true labor of love, and it took many minds to come together as one. My thanks go out to all of you. I knew that there were more heads hungry for something like this. We're living in a special time in history. We have seen hip-hop grow up alongside of us, even if we are somewhat confused by its growth at times. Many of us look back to a golden age, holding onto strong memories. Yet, our ears remain receptive to new sounds. We'll properly archive the history while we keep a close eye on the future history-makers. In 1974, there was no such thing as a hip-hop record. Hip-hop was Kool Herc rocking doubles of "Apache"—no MC—just a DJ and two turntables. We hope to put the DJ back at the center of hip-hop from a historical perspective, and demonstrate that DJing and record collecting gave birth to hip-hop as we now know it. We dig into the lives of the creators of the funky breaks, and the music beyond, both old and new. We tie together the divergent aspects of hip-hop culture with the arts at large and give you a fresh perspective you won't find anywhere else. We shed light on aspects of the culture that truly matter, the true essence of creativity, not the trappings of it. Wax Poetics is for the collector that, years from now, will pull out an issue and still find it relevant to their life, much like the vinyl we all love. In time, your collection will be a set of reference guides to deepen your understanding of the music and culture. Wax Poetics is the light on the path of funk and rhythm—walk with us.

Peace,

Andre Torres
Editor-in-Chief

waxpoetics

Editor-in-Chief/Publisher	Andre Torres
Senior Editor	Brian DiGenti
Creative Director	Kevin DeBernardi
Editorial Councelor	John Paul Jones
Contributing Editors	Dante Carfagna
	Andrew Mason
Production Assistants	Lance Guerriere
	Greg DiGenti
Marketing Director	Steven Mark Klein
Accounts Manager	Joy Blameuser

Contributing Writers — Eothen Alapatt, Joe Allen, Chris Aylen, Jon Azpiri, Cosmo Baker, Wilson Brooks, Chad Burnett, Dante Carfagna, Thomas Gesthuizen, Steven Hager, Reeve Hohlt, John Paul Jones, Wilson F. Karaman, Joe Keilch, Daniel Gray-Kontar, Andrew Mason, Todd Shanker, Oliver Wang, Zaid

Contributing Photographers — Wilson Brooks, Chad Burnett, John Carluccio, Beth Fladung, Thomas Gesthuizen, Bryan Hitch, Monika Magiera, Andrew Mason, Jessica Miller, Prince Paul, Michael Spears

Contributing Artists — Chris Aylen, John Carluccio, Andrew Robinson

Special thanks to:

The Blameuser Family, the DeBernardi Family, the DiGenti Family, and the Torres Family. Kane and Mao. Ed Applewhite. Language. Rich Medina. Ross Schwartzman. Caroline Robbins. Jeff Chang. Troy Smith. Raymond @ *URB*. Mark Pollard @ *Stealth*. Monica Hernandez @ *Color Lines*. Laris @ *Sound Collector*. Steven Hager. Infamous @ *Tablist*. Monica Lynch. DJ Atsushi. Chioke Kendrick. Underground Railroad. Eric Ducker @ *The Fader*. Amala and Scribe @ the Jump Off. Yasuhiro Yamashita. *Big Daddy*, Keith Williams, and Steve Kader. Zaid would like to thank Fin Gooding for the hook-up; Wilson Karaman would like to thank Clive Chin and Earl Morgan for graciously agreeing to be interviewed. Ira, Malcolm, and Ras Kush (Jammyland). Celine Kagan (for the edu-ma-cation), Lauren Danza, Eli Mavros, Jane, and Joe; Rehash would like to thank John Doe (for the "KC Stomp" info), and most importantly thanks to Dr. Mack, a man who has stood the test of time, and as a musician remains determined—Wax Poetics is extremely grateful for his participation and wishes him the very best. Our writers, artists, and photographers who dig deep and bring with them a passion for the music, which shows in their efforts. Our advertisers who believe in us enough to join us, our retailers, distributors, and readers the world over.

ISBN 978-0-9992127-9-0
© 2002, 2020 Wax Poetics

Originally published Spring 2002

Published by Wax Poetics Books
Printed by Lightning Source

All rights reserved.
Unauthorized duplication without prior written consent is prohibited.

The Academic Archive: Vol 2

by Joe Allen

"If God were a DJ, he'd be Harry Smith"

Folk singer Peter Stampfel's claim about Harry Smith is startling for a number of reasons. Smith was not an old school DJ overlooked by hip-hop history, nor the latest turntable prodigy. In fact, he was not really a DJ at all. His work, though, anticipated much of the culture of beatdigging—from *Ultimate Breaks & Beats* through *The Funky 16 Corners*. Smith redefined the role of the record collector—part DJ, artist, historian, archaeologist, and curator—painstakingly collecting the rarest of records, researching the long-forgotten artists, and then carefully sequencing and collating the best of his collection.

In 1997, Smithsonian Folkways reissued Harry Smith's *Anthology of American Folk Music* on six CDs, complete with Smith's original detailed handbook to the collection, and an extensive booklet of contemporary "essays, appreciations, and annotations." The *Anthology*, eighty-four tracks originally spread out on three double LPs in 1952 on Folkways Records, centers on the years 1927–1932. Beginning with the advent of accurate recording technology and ending with the Depression's ruination of the music business, these years represent the pinnacle of what Smith broadly defined as folk music. Much like the preponderance of rare 45s from the early '70s, his choices often initially saw limited pressing, maybe 500 copies mostly restricted to a certain locality—he even located some in Salvation Army shops and others in warehouses as they were cleared for military use in WWII.

By the mid-1940s, Harry Smith had already established himself as a legendary collector of folk, blues, jazz, country, gospel, and other uniquely American styles of music from the early twentieth century. "He was reputed to have one of the finest, not the biggest, record collections that people knew," said fellow collector Luis Kemnitzer. Smith was protective of his collection and almost greedy for additional rare records because he felt that his record collection would, as Kemnitzer notes, "go to an institution and be curated."[1] Beyond the healthy competition for obscure records, Kemnitzer and Smith shared in the musicology:

> We shared a love for the records themselves as well as the music that was encoded in them. The labels, the record jackets, the catalogs, and the announcements from the early '30s and before were sensual tokens of the eras, and we felt, saw, and smelled what the music was expressing.

Smith ultimately did something unconventional with his archaeology of music, which had been for the most part out of circulation for twenty years or so; he released three volumes of the *Anthology of American Folk Music* in 1952.

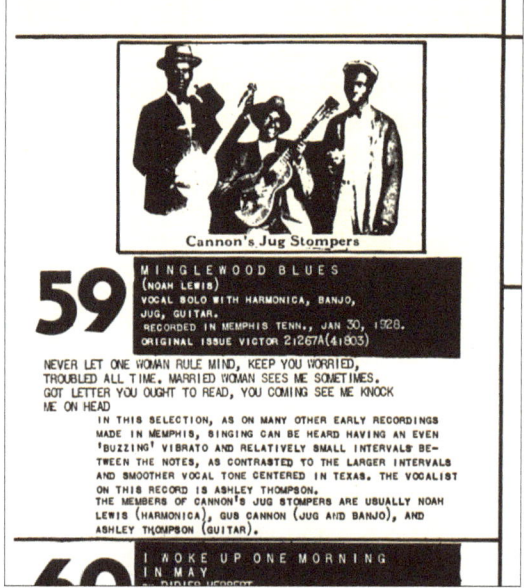

His accompanying handbook included a wealth of material: annotations for each song, an exhaustive cross-index to the songs, a bibliography of sources, and a diverse array of photos, record covers, woodcuts, and quotes. The strikingly large numbering which labeled each annotation **1** through **84** indicated the important placement of each song. The three volumes were already grouped—*Ballads*, *Social Music*, and *Songs*—yet the numbering and annotations in the booklet ran through all three volumes. The visual boldness of the numbers exemplifies one of Smith's most significant purposes—like any masterful DJ, he laboriously sequenced the tracks in this particular order. The tracks seamlessly blend into one another as melodies, instrumentation, motifs, and images connect the *Anthology* track to track, genre to genre, volume to volume, "as if," according to musicologist Greil Marcus, "some grand system lurked within the elements Smith had brought to bear upon each other." Think of the diversity collected on the *Ultimate Breaks & Beats* series and the many ways the beats can be fluidly mixed together (and especially Bambaataa's record collection and his early mixes). John Fahey, a renowned guitarist, concludes, "Smith had an encyclopedic knowledge of 78s and a preternatural feel for the connection between them—across race and ethnic boundaries—not only to codify them for us but also to have this collection persist as an absolutely definitive and essential historical document."

Smith also took advantage of the available technology, as Smithsonian Folkways curator Anthony Seeger states, "The LP medium was fairly new in 1952, when the *Anthology* was first released. The LP (33⅓ RPM 12-inch disc) made it possible to assemble a long, unbroken sequence of songs together; before this, a single song per side was the standard." If only Smith had a crossfader at his disposal… Nonetheless, in a sense, the three volumes of the original *Anthology* appear to be the first series of mixtapes of the twentieth century. Luc Sante, a collector and friend of Smith, now calls the *Anthology* a "work of art, rounded and complete unto itself…a brilliant montage…an essential element of American culture."

At the time of the *Anthology's* release, many listeners became active participants in what publisher Jon Pankake has called the "brotherhood of the anthology." The *Anthology* documented an underground of folk music very different from the folk music easily available at the time, so when listeners like Pankake became spellbound by the *Anthology*, they wanted more information about the eclectic mix of artists and began tracking down more of their original recordings. After twenty years of collecting possibly even rarer recordings, Pankake claims his collection approximated a "cosmic version of the *Anthology*"—compare our record collections to *Ultimate Breaks & Beats*. *Anthology* listeners became "anthologists" themselves. Pankake remarks:

My own search eventually drew me into the netherworld of collector's newsletters, record auction lists, jazz and blues scholarship, mimeographed ephemera, and cranky antiquarian collectors knowledgeable about the history of the recording industry.

Pankake's extensive newsletter, *The Little Sandy Review*, included features on *Anthology* artists, record reviews, and other commentary on the 1960s folk revival. The *Review* helped form a national network of collectors who readily traded reel-to-reel dubs of scarce 78s. Because of his appreciation of the music and his desire to have exhaustive discographies, Pankake readily traded his want list and have list with collectors from coast to coast. Collectors who traveled to the deep south in search of dusty 78s marginalized Pankake for just collecting dubs. Renowned 78 collector Joe Bussard was, as Pankake explained to me, "very scornful of the dubs…He was especially interested in the artifacts."[2] Their authentic artifact versus reel-to-reel dub debate anticipates the original pressing versus reissue discussion of today. Nonetheless, since exhaustive discographies for *Anthology* artists were not available in the early 1960s when Pankake and others were trading dubs, collectors like him codified and documented an era of music that might have been buried and lost.

The recent reissue of Harry Smith's *Anthology* has generated a renewed interest in American roots music. Techno-savant Moby, so taken with the *Anthology*, decided to sample a number of blues, folk, and gospel songs for his 1999 release *Play*. The scope of the *Anthology* mines an emotional landscape and an array of sounds rarely touched by hip-hop; however, if Moby can successfully incorporate the dusty sounds of the late 1920s and early 1930s into his techno-driven beats, hip-hop producers should take note. The massive expanse of early American blues, folk, gospel, and country might be the last largely untouched and unsampled field of twentieth-century American music. At the very least, Harry Smith's mix warrants a careful listen.

Joe Allen *teaches English at Dutchess Community College in Poughkeepsie, NY.*

Notes:

1. This and subsequent quotes regarding Smith's *Anthology* appear in "A Booklet of Essays, Appreciations, and Annotations Pertaining to the *Anthology of American Folk Music* edited by Harry Smith" (Smithsonian Folkways Recordings 1997).

2. Author's interview with Jon Pankake, February 25, 2002.

Artwork reprinted with permission.

Afterward:

Musicologist Neil Rosenberg adds new and updated annotations to each of the eighty-four songs in Smith's *Anthology*, not to replace Smith's own annotations but to supplement them. In his introductory essay, Rosenberg discusses one more connection to beatdigging culture: "Like many reissues of old 78s in the post-war years by independent companies, Smith's anthology was a 'pirate'—the recordings were not licensed from the original manufacturers; the performers were not paid for their use. Initially, Folkways owner Moe Asch felt this was unnecessary, believing the companies had given up their rights by destroying the masters and not keeping the recordings in print. Ultimately Folkways did license some of the recordings and, with this reissue [the six-CD box set], all are licensed."

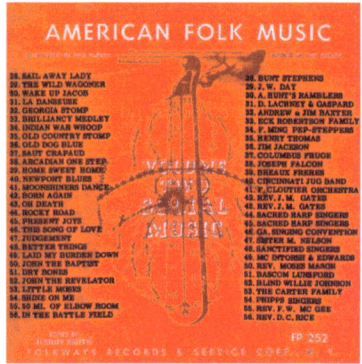

Pretty Purdie

by
Eothen Alapatt

photos by
Beth Fladung

I've known Bernard since about 1966. I was sixteen when I met him. As a musician, Bernard came along when the music changed. Before him the beat relied on the shuffle. Purdie came along with a straight eight-beat—with the shuffle on the inside. See what I'm saying? And the sound just changed. He also came along when the electric bass came in. After '64, you didn't see acoustic basses with R&B groups. As the bass got more projection—and louder—the drummer could afford to be louder. And Purdie certainly was louder than any of those other cats that were down there! He had a strong, strong foot and a strong, strong beat that was perfect for the bass guitar.

What a person plays means nothing if the time's no good, and Purdie is the king of time. The naval observatory can get their time from Purdie. They gotta call him! That's why me and him hit it off right away. When I first came down and hit the scene I was known as a very busy bass player. Not busy in terms of work, but busy in terms of notes! Mostly what I learned from Purdie was what *not* to play. I saw how Purdie would build a song. A little bit here, a little more next time around, throw your little zinger in here but don't overshadow the rest of the rhythm section. He played like a boxer in a boxing match. A boxer doesn't come out swinging like crazy at the opening bell; he picks [his opponent] apart gradually. That's what I learned from Purdie. He's the master of building.

He is worth everything that everybody says about him. He's the man. In that particular groove of music, he *is* the man and *has been* and *always* will be. In the vein of music that you call rhythm and blues, I don't think I've ever come across anyone that is his equal. When he's in his element, forget about it!

I believe everything that we hear today, no matter what it is, came from what Purdie set up.

—Wilbur "Bad" Bascomb, as told to Eothen Alapatt. 3/4/02

Eothen: You know, even though I've known you for quite some time, I don't think I've ever read any interviews with you. Most of the information I have on you comes from the back cover of the *Shapes of Rhythm* LP! For instance, your birthplace…

Bernard Purdie: I was born in Elkton, Maryland—the seat of Cecil County. Maryland has twenty-three counties. Cecil County is one of them. Elkton is the biggest of the small, little towns, and that's where all the politicians and banks are. It's there that everybody comes to. It's also the place that had one [institution] where all the Black kids went to school, which is George Washington Carver. Every Black kid in Cecil County was bussed to the Black school. It was right near my home—a mile away actually—in Elkton. My family walked to school.

Was Elkton a cultural, as well as political, center? Did you grow up around music?

No, there were no musicians around me. I'm sorry—there was one, and he had a band. The Clyde Bessick Orchestra. This was jazz, but it was called "big band" at the time. It was called "dance music." I was five or six when I first took notice. I started playing with the band at age eight. My teacher at GWC, Leonard Haywood, was the drummer with the orchestra.

So you played in the school band, and Haywood was your instructor?

He wouldn't let me in the band at first. [*laughs*] I'm very serious. It wasn't so much that I wasn't good enough, it was about an age situation. I was too young to be in the band, but I was gifted enough to play. So in order to do what I did, he would allow me to be in the band only if I took up another instrument.

Which was?

The trumpet. The worst thing he could possibly do to me.

Why?

[*laughs*] Because I couldn't stand the trumpet! From trumpet I had to go play flute for a year and a half. I was seven or eight at the time. See, I always had rhythm on the drums. But he wouldn't let me touch the drums at school—he would only let me do it at his house. So I would go to his house, while he was teaching other students, and sit on the steps watching him teach other students. When he wanted an example, I'd jump up to do it. He would tell me to sit down and play what he wanted, then I would get [off the drum kit] and sit back on the steps. This went on for almost seven years.

Why did you go along with this? Most kids would have given up!

I always wanted to play the drums. I wasn't gonna let no one stop me from playing the drums. But Mr. Haywood had me play the trumpet and the flute because he wanted me to learn music. But I didn't know that. I thought he was punishing me!

How fortunate that he started you on the path to becoming a musical drummer.

Of course it is, when you realize that twenty or thirty years later.

It takes a hip teacher to instill that musicality in you, without you even knowing what he was doing.

He was quite the hip teacher. Oh, he saw the gift. I had the gift. And that's what he used to say to me. I would get so upset, 'cause I thought that he was saying that to get me to shut up. You know, there were so many little things that he would say and do, but he never raised his voice. That's the thing that got to me. I would get mad and upset, and he would tell me, "You're still going to have to do it." I would say, "Why, why? No one else has to do it. And I'm better than any of the other students you have. I can play rings around them!" He would say something like, "Yeah, but they're older." He always had an excuse.

Ah, the infamous Bernard Purdie self-confidence rears its head at an early age!

Oh, my confidence was there when I was four or five.

You said you played in Bessick's orchestra at age eight. So Mr. Haywood must have taken your latent abilities seriously.

Oh yes. I played on the bandstand. The reason is that every Friday and Saturday, Mr. Haywood had to play with the band. And he would get drunk. See, he liked vodka or gin. And he would give me this tall glass, supposedly filled with water, and I would hold it for him. And I would feed him from this glass, which was full of either vodka or gin. And it was great. [*laughs*] Because when the intermission came, he would sweat so much that he would go out to his station wagon, and he'd sit down and fall asleep. So I would finish the job. I would go back, and sit down, finish the job—[and everyone in the band] would know he was too drunk to continue.

Wow!

Yeah. I knew all of the Bessick songs. Every one of them. Because I knew everything Mr. Haywood did. I could mimic him with no problem. But it wasn't about mimicking. He wanted me to learn music. So I knew how to play—and interpret—whatever I sat down to do.

When did you form your first band?

I had my band when I was twelve years old. That was Jackie Lee and the Angels. I was the leader, even though my name wasn't Jackie Lee. I was definitely an Angel. [*laughs*] I also signed the contracts.

A businessman at age twelve?

Oh yeah, you had to be! The thing is, these are the things Mr. Haywood taught me as I was growing up. You had to learn how to manage. And I'm not just talking about managing money. I never looked at it as managing money. But managing to do the *job*. It was always a job. No matter what happened, I had to do the job. Now when I got paid …The first time I got paid, I became a professional. The first time I got paid, it was either eight or ten dollars. That was big money! I mean, that was super money and I got paid to play the music. I was eleven or twelve.

So by the time you formed the Angels, you were quite the young veteran.

Oh yes. I would always be around for the Clyde Bessick Orchestra, and I was also playing in the high school band. This went on till the end of the '50s.

Then you enrolled at Morgan State University.

Well, I was out of school for a few months 'cause I couldn't afford to go anywhere. So two members of the House of Delegates—Mr. Berkely and Mr. Stanley—got me into college. They knew me 'cause I worked for them in Elkton. But I had to go to study business administration. The reason was that this was the only opening they had, so that's how they got me in. It had nothing to do with what I really wanted to do, but it was a way to get me into the school. They had a great music program at Morgan, one of the best in the world. I could only take one music class though. At first I could only do my major, my minor had to wait for at least a year.

But you must have at least joined the college band.

Yeah. I joined the band immediately. They knew that I could play. They also knew that I was good at what I did. We had two brothers there—I'm trying to think of their names. They played trombone and trumpet. Boy, they were awesome! They had their own band as well, so I joined. But I didn't know that they were either alcoholics or drug addicts. Turned out they did both. But they were phenomenal musicians, and everyone around town knew them 'cause they were in their second or third years of college.

Sounds like you were a busy man.

I was also one of the photographers for all the freshman. And I worked in the cafeteria, 'cause I was there on a workman's scholarship. So I had to do those things, as well as excel in my studies.

You were hustling.

Well, you had to! That was the only way to get ahead! Outside of school, I was playing swing, the blues, R&B, country…Whatever was necessary for me to do. And I started forming and playing in different bands. Within six months of being at Morgan, I was playing in three different bands.

I was playing uptown, at the nightclubs. I could also play show music, 'cause I read music!

Thanks to Mr. Haywood.

Right. It was all easy for me to do. Because of that, I did what was necessary. That's when I ran into a man named Purnell Rice. He was the only drummer I ever knew that could play a roll on a pillow. He wasn't allowed to make noise in his house, so he learned how to practice on a pillow. I saw it with my own eyes, I couldn't believe it. I knew then I had to go back to the woodshed! [*laughs*]

How so?

That man's hands were so fast! He was much older than me; I would say he was as much as fifteen years older than me. He was playing strip music, all kinds of show music, anything that had to do with reading and interpreting music for people who danced.

So he was an inspiration during your college years?

He made me want to go practice. I could play the precision drumming, 'cause I played in the circus band when I was fourteen. That was never my problem. But I was never super fast. My speed to make the rolls…I couldn't do the rolls anywhere near the way Mr. Rice could do them. He did the press roll like he was taking a piece of paper and ripping it—he was so smooth. But for me…"Your rolls are always like biscuits," he used to tell me. My rolls were a bit…

Slower?

Well, they were never super smooth. I had to do what they called the "buzz roll." But I would never be as smooth as him. To this day, I still do biscuits. Oh yeah, I love my biscuits. 'Cause they work for me. I don't try to be no super smooth cat! My little biscuits work!

When did you graduate from Morgan?

I only had two years at Morgan. I didn't graduate 'cause I left and came to New York City in 1961. The band that I had, we had been playing well together. Everything worked out, and [the band members] wanted to go to New York to make a record. It was there that I met and worked with Mickey and Sylvia. We rerecorded "Love Is Strange" for their own label. That was my first session date, one week after moving to New York. I was living in the Bronx.

And you never left.

I mean, I got here, had a ball, and fell in love with this town. I was just a kid. I just loved what I saw.

Not to mention you had solid work lined up!

Man, Mickey and Sylvia paid me eighty dollars to work from noon until four o'clock on a Sunday. I got paid eighty dollars! I was rich! I was *rich*! I knew I was rich. I'd hit the big time. I went back to the Comet Club, where I was working nights, at 165th and Washington. We played for the door. And of course, I made all kinds of tips, 'cause I sang and danced as well. I did everything. That was what it was. I was a showman.

And then the session work started pouring in.

That all happened from demos. There was a guy named Herb Abramson. He, I found out later, was the president of Atlantic Records. I met him 'cause he had a recording studio on the sixth floor up on 56th Street. I just went and introduced myself. I would go around and tell people, "I'm good. Hire me."

So the stories of you walking around, wearing the signs that read, "'Pretty' Purdie, the hit-maker…"

…All of them are true. I know now that I'm a master of self-promotion. But back then I'd just go ask anyone to give me a job! [*laughs*]

Like Rick Shorter.

I got in on the ground floor of New York sessioning. Rick was another person doing demos. By 1964, I had a reputation. I had made hit records! "Just One Look," Les Cooper's "Wiggle Wobble," "Hi Heeled Sneakers." That's how I met Galt [MacDermot]. That was the same year, 1964.

Do you remember the day that you two met?

Of course I remember meeting him! [*laughs*] The day that I met him—the strangest part is that I'm looking at him, and talking to him, and I remember saying to him, "Do you know what you're doing? Do you know what kind of music you're doing here?" He said [calmly], "Yes." I said, "But, do you *really* know what kind of music this is?" And he said [calmly], "Yes." I said, "But how would you know how to do this kind of music? I mean, this is African music, and funk, and pop—all in one!" I said, "I don't really think you know what you're doing! And if you do, that would make you a genius."

And?

He said, "Well I *do* know what I'm doing." I said what I said because I really didn't think he understood. Man, *impressed* isn't the word. I was floored. I'm telling you, I didn't understand that the man really knew what he was doing.

Yeah, I've seen the pictures! By looking at Galt, you wouldn't be able to tell that he was such a musical revolutionary.

I had never seen a white guy play that good—with sincerity—and know exactly what he wanted. He knew exactly what he wanted and this is what he asked for [on demo sessions]. So I said, "Okay, I'll do it."

You two got along well?

We hit it off *immediately*. Absolutely immediately. At that time I was arrogant, but I didn't know I was arrogant. I thought I was just smart. He told me that I was arrogant. But I'm playing the music he asked for. He told me I was the first one to give him exactly what he asked for.

Can you clarify?

For me, I always had to play what was being dictated. That's how I learned to play. But this is where my gift comes in. My gift allows me to play anything with anybody, 'cause I hear where they want to go with their music.

Galt was perhaps the first person to document you as a musician—to focus on your abilities—with his *Shapes of Rhythm* album in 1966. That was an album made by sessioners—Galt, yourself, Jimmy Lewis on bass, and "Snag" Allen on guitar—for themselves.

Yeah! I remember that record. Galt would play some of a tune on the piano. I would turn around and say something to Jimmy—but I had to learn to keep my mouth shut; Jimmy actually threatened me a couple of times. Oh yeah! Jimmy would cut you or shoot you, it didn't matter which. He pulled his gun on me once! I'm telling you, that cat always had a gun and a knife. He was from the streets! [*laughs*] He was a street person.

Sounds like those must have been some stressful sessions.

No, not really. The sessions weren't volatile. Galt was the soothing image for everything. And Snag always said, "Yeah, sure man. Let's do it." Snag would do the backbeats, then play a rhythm afterwards. We always did what Galt wanted. Jimmy was the one who took longer to get it done. But eventually, since he listened to what Galt was doing on the piano, he would give in. That's why I would say to Galt, "You're either a genius, or you're crazy."

I think that "Coffee Cold," one of Galt's tunes that you recorded during the *Shapes of Rhythm* session, is a little of both. The rhythm on that song is far beyond the conventions of the time.

Oh yes, I remember that song. But the point is, I got that feel from Galt. Listen to what I'm saying to you, he was playing those types of rhythms on the piano. And these were African rhythms. This is why I didn't understand—why everybody didn't understand—what he was doing. He was playing African rhythms! After working with him for a year I discovered that he'd been living in Africa! I never thought to ask! Never even occurred to me to ask if he'd lived in Africa. All I knew is that he played [African rhythms] on the piano. And I said, "Okay, if this is what you want, I'll play it." You never expect to see someone—he had gray hair then—to play these kind of rhythms. How would he know?

As the '60s progress, you play drums on records that have influenced drummers from then until now. Like Aretha Franklin's "Rock Steady," and King Curtis's live version of "Memphis Soul Stew."

Well, I agree with you there. I'm learning that that's what [my drumming] has done. But to me it was just a job. When Aretha sat down at the piano, the whole arrangement was coming out of that piano, from her fingers. I just took it out. I just gave parts to different people in the band.

As one of the pillars of funk drumming in America, when did you realize that the funk rhythm had taken over American popular music?

I never looked at anything as being taken over. People misunderstand. I had no idea that I was setting a trend of any kind. I was just doing a job. It was just a job to me. This is what the person was playing, I was bringing out the rhythm. It was a job!

You were damn good at your job. It didn't matter if you played rock, folk, funk, or jazz—any record that you're a part of rings with your unique sound.

The drumming I played was simple to me, 'cause it was part of what the music was supposed to sound like. I know that people are saying all these fabulous things about me—that I changed the world, and this and that. Eothen, it was a job. [*laughs*] I could not tell you that what I was about to play was going to change the music business. You get these ideas…They come from somebody, from someplace. They were not my ideas in the first place. I took what people had and made it work. That's what I was great at.

In the last issue, we interviewed your contemporary, Idris Muhammad. He said that you took a hi-hat lick from him.

[*laughs*] No, that's not quite so. I was doing that [lick] when I was twelve years old. I was doing that with the big band. It is my trademark. I was doing that in a fourteen-piece orchestra. My teacher, Mr. Haywood, told me what I was playing was eventually going to happen in music. "But not now!" he'd shout. "Don't do it now! Leave it alone!" [*laughs*] I didn't know what I was doing. I had to figure out what I was doing.

No matter how progressive your drumming became, you never left the pocket. I'm thinking of your drum breaks recorded on songs like Charles Kynard's "Sweetheart." You stay in the groove, and we love you for it.

You had to. All my life, I was told, "Do not break the rhythm. Let people dance." That is why my solos are the way they are, I tried to make them danceable. I was trying to keep the music as tight as possible, without making big splashes or getting in the way. I didn't want to get in the way of the vocalist, but, yet, inspire the vocalist. I did that because I learned how to control my beats.

Speaking of beats, your first album on Date is full of 'em!

Mmm hmm! My manager at the time, Dave Kirkpatrick, was the vice president of Epic Records. At that time, I was producing for him, for Daedalus Productions. I did Peaches and Herb, Ronnie Dyson—and we also had Sly and the Family Stone. As quiet [as it] was kept, it wasn't Sly that was producing the records. For example, his first album—the only one that was a happening album—I did that for Daedalus. I didn't know I was supposed to get credit for these things. Ken Williams and myself, we had to fix Sly's albums because he was tore up the whole time he was in the studio doing these things. We had to make his records happen.

How exactly would you "fix" his albums?

We would switch things over to 8-track or 12-track. Keep what he had, and add little things to help support and to keep the music happening. I did the same thing [for] the Beatles.

You know, I'm sure Sly fans are going to contest your claim—much like the Beatles fans have contested you since you came forth a few years ago to dash their perceptions of their musical heroes!

Oh yeah. And you want to know what? I don't care anymore! About the Beatles situation? That was part of my job. I was the fixer! I've been fixing things since 1963.

Any other notable projects that you "fixed?"

We had the same thing with Eric Burdon and the Animals. Just about every European act that was being done in the '60s and the early part of the '70s.

How about the Monkees?

Yes, the Monkees. Of course! The guy who was their contractor was a drummer. But he stayed drunk all the time.

And alongside of all this, you found time to revolutionize both the sound and feel of funk drumming.

But I had a good engineer, see. Phil Ramone. He liked the idea of the echo chamber. We used an echo chamber, and we studied where to place the mic in relation to the snare drum. He kept the mic at a small distance from the drum, but he used the room itself as its own echo chamber.

Yeah, hearing you on your early records—and even the jazz dates you did for Bob Porter—you get the feel that you're seven feet tall!

Exactly. It's booming, but the looseness is what gives it the flow, and the feel to stay out of everybody else's way.

Were all of your solo ventures as successful as the session dates you did?

Yes, all of them were. I had good arrangers. I always had good arrangers with me. I would give them what I wanted, and then I'd let them fatten up what I had—with whatever they wanted to do.

Tell me about what has to be your most obscure release, the soundtrack to *Lialeh*.

[*laughs*] That was the first time I was going to have credit as a writer/composer. It was a small-scale movie; I scored the entire thing. We had ten thousand copies manufactured, and then they told me I couldn't do any more. They had to come to me to get my permission every time they were going to make a deal around the world. The ten thousand [pressed domestically] were made by my own company, which was Poor Boy Records. I sure wish I had kept some copies!

You know, an interesting parallel between the recording trajectory of both Idris and yourself emerges in the mid- to late '70s, with disco. I would have thought that since you are both such rhythmic drummers, you two would have fought against the disco feel. Instead you assimilated it.

When music is changing, and the feel of the music is changing, you go along with it. You don't try to fight it. You can still make rhythm out of disco, but it's all about *how* you do *what* you do *when* you play. In the late '70s, I went along with the program. I kept it tight, kept it funky, and then I loosened it up. Let the music breathe.

And the '80s?

The '80s were very horrible, but I was playing live. I was playing jazz with Dizzy Gillespie all over the world. I was with Gato Barbieri, I was with Roy Ayers, and then back with Aretha. I always thought back to the '60s and '70s, but I never let it interfere with the job I was called to do. You go and do your job. In the '80s, though, I learned how to use the computer. I was writing music with, and without, the computer.

In the late '80s, hip-hop sampling brought your drumming back to the forefront of popular music.

In the beginning I didn't take to it too well, 'cause Aretha got paid, or James Brown got paid. I had to accept the fact that I wasn't going to get paid, 'cause I wasn't the artist being sampled. I was the drummer. In the beginning I was upset, now…nah. No one can take away from me what I have, what I've learned, and what I've done. And I don't care what they try to do. The point is I've been able to survive all of these years. Over forty years in this business. I was able to learn the business, and play and survive in the business.

And the hip-hop generation regards you as one of the godfathers of the movement, much like James Brown.

I realize that now. That is a big thing to me now. I'm very pleased. This is why I'm working. I know what I'm going to do for the next six months. I'm running all over the world. I'm teaching, I'm giving lectures, I'm giving master classes, and I'm traveling around the world having a good time. Traveling two hundred and fifty thousand miles a year and loving it. And getting paid. I figure I have another twenty-five to thirty years. Oh, at least!

Ah, the regenerative powers of music…

You have to regenerate! You got to! I've only noticed my impact in the past fifteen years. And I'm beginning to enjoy what it's done for me. I don't have to go around patting myself on the back for my achievements. They're now being put in front of my face. And other people around the world are beginning to see what I've achieved. Which is why they've kept me working. This is my way of getting paid. But I also know that I have to give back. And as long as I feel that way, I'll still be compensated. I don't have a problem in the world when it comes down to playing this music. I've been very lucky and fortunate with my arthritis and stuff like that. I'm going to go ahead and enjoy myself. And love it. Absolutely love it. Yes, it was a job. It will always be a job. But…I can have fun…with my job. ○

Since last issue, Eothen Alapatt *has spent six weeks touring England and Europe in support of his compilation,* The Funky 16 Corners *(Stones Throw). Now back in Los Angeles, he's concentrating on Stones Throw's hip-hop releases, and planning the launch of a subsidiary label to house his reissue projects.*

Bernard "Pretty" Purdie Selected Discography

Soul Drums (Date 1967)
Purdie Good (Prestige 1971)
Stand by Me (Whatcha See Is Whatcha Get) (Mega 1971)
Soul Is…Pretty Purdie (Flying Dutchman 1972)
Shaft (Prestige 1972)
Lialeh (Original Movie Soundtrack) (Bryan 1974)
Coolin' 'n Groovin' (West 47th 1995)
In Tokyo (West 47th 1995)
Master Drummers, Volume 1 (Luv n' Haight 1995)
Master Drummers, Volume 2 (Ubiquity 1996)
Bernard Purdie's Soul to Jazz (Act 1996)
Bernard Purdie's Soul to Jazz II (Act 1997)
King of the Beat (2002)

Harold Alexander *Sunshine Man* (Flying Dutchman 1971)
Harold Alexander *Are You Ready?* (Flying Dutchman 1972)
Gene Ammons *The Boss Is Back* (Prestige 1969)
Gene Ammons *Brother Jug!* (Prestige 1970)
Louis Armstrong *Louis Armstrong and His Friends* (Flying Dutchman 1970)
Roy Ayers Ubiquity *Change Up the Groove* (Polydor 1974)
Roy Ayers Ubiquity *A Tear to a Smile* (Polydor 1975)
Roy Ayers Ubiquity *Vibrations* (Polydor 1976)
Albert Ayler *New Grass* (Impulse! 1968)
Bama the Village Poet *Ghettos of My Mind* (Aware 1974)
Gato Barbieri *El Gato* (Flying Dutchman 1971)
Salome Bey *Sings Songs from Dude* (Kilmarnock 1973)
Michael Bolotin *Self-Titled* (RCA 1975)
Randy Brecker *Score* (Solid State 1969)
Charlie Brown *Why Is Everybody Always Pickin' on Me* (Contact 1972)
James Brown *It's a Man's Man's Man's World* (King 1966)
James Brown *Say It Loud, I'm Black and I'm Proud* (King 1969)
James Brown *Get on the Good Foot* (Polydor 1972)
Oscar Brown *Movin' On* (Atlantic 1972)
Rusty Bryant *Night Train Now!* (Prestige 1969)
Rusty Bryant *Until It's Time For You to Go* (Prestige 1974)
Buari *Self-Titled* (RCA 1975)
Gary Burton *Good Vibes* (Atlantic 1970)
Billy Butler *Plays Via Galactica* (Kilmarnock 1973)
Charlie Byrd *The Great Byrd* (Columbia 1969)
Charlie Byrd *Aquarius* (Columbia 1971)
Bobby Callendar *Rainbow* (Boston Sound 1969)
Larry Coryell *Coryell* (Vanguard 1969)
Larry Coryell *Fairyland* (Mega 1971)
Joe Cocker *Luxury You Can Afford* (A&M 1978)
Hank Crawford *It's a Funky Thing to Do* (Atlantic/Cotillion 1970)
Hank Crawford *Help Me Make It Through the Night* (KUDU 1972)
Hank Crawford *Don't You Worry 'Bout a Thing* (KUDU 1974)
Hank Crawford *I Hear a Symphony* (KUDU 1975)
Eddie Curtis *Eddie Curtis and All those Cats* (Shere Khan)
Wild Bill Davis *Doin' His Thing* (RCA 1967)
Miles Davis *Get Up With It* (Columbia 1975)
Wayne Davis *A View From Another Place* (Atlantic 1973)
Lou Donaldson *Sweet Lou* (Blue Note 1974)
Cornell Dupree *Teasin'* (Atlantic 1974)
The Dynamic 3B's *After Hours With the 3B's* (3B's 1993)
Pee Wee Ellis *Home in the Country* (Savoy 1977)
Roberta Flack *Quiet Fire* (Atlantic 1971)
Roberta Flack & Donny Hathaway *Self-Titled* (Atlantic 1972)
Sonny Forriest *Tuff Pickin'* (Decca)
Ronnie Foster *Sweet Revival* (Blue Note 1973)
Aretha Franklin *Young, Gifted & Black* (Atlantic 1971)
Aretha Franklin *Let Me in Your Life* (Atlantic 1974)

Aretha Franklin *With Everything I Feel in Me* (Atlantic 1974)
Caesar Frazier *'75* (Westbound 1975)
Nikki Giovanni *The Way I Feel* (Niktom)
Benny Golson *Tune In, Turn On* (Verve 1967)
Daryl Hall/John Oates *Abandoned Luncheonette* (Atlantic 1973)
Herbie Hancock *Fat Albert Rotunda* (WB 1969)
Ellerine Harding *Ellerine* (Mainstream 1972)
Eddie Harris & Les McCann *Second Movement* (Atlantic 1971)
Richard "Groove" Holmes *Night Glider* (Groove Merchant 1973)
Richard "Groove" Holmes *New Groove* (Groove Merchant)
John Lee Hooker *Simply the Truth* (One Way 1969)
Freddie Hubbard *A Soul Experiment* (Atlantic 1969)
The Insect Trust *Self-Titled* (Capitol 1968)
The Insect Trust *Hoboken Saturday Night* (Atco 1970)
Dizzy Gillespie *Cornucopia* (Solid State 1970)
"Boogaloo" Joe Jones *Boogaloo Joe* (Prestige 1969)
"Boogaloo" Joe Jones *Right On, Brother!* (Prestige 1970)
"Boogaloo" Joe Jones *No Way!* (Prestige 1971)
"Boogaloo" Joe Jones *What It Is* (Prestige 1972)
Quincy Jones *Walking in Space* (A&M 1969)
Quincy Jones *Body Heat* (A&M 1974)
Artie Kaplan *Confessions of a Male Chauvinist Pig* (Vanguard 1972)
King Curtis *Live at Fillmore West* (Atco 1971)
King Curtis *Everybody's Talkin'* (Atco 1972)
King Curtis & the Kingpins *Self-Titled* (Atco)
B.B. King *Completely Well* (ABC 1970)
B.B. King *Guess Who* (MCA 1972)
Rahsaan Roland Kirk *Blacknuss* (Atlantic 1971)
Al Kooper *You Never Know Who Your Friends Are* (Columbia 1969)
Charles Kynard *Reelin' with the Feelin'* (Prestige 1969)
Charles Kynard *Afro-Disiac* (Prestige 1970)
Charles Kynard *Wa-Tu-Wa-Zui* (Prestige 1970)
The Last Poets *Delights of the Garden* (Douglas/Casablanca 1977)
Yusef Lateef *Yusef Lateef's Detroit* (Atlantic 1969)
Yusef Lateef *The Diverse Lateef* (Atlantic)
Lightnin' Rod *Hustler's Convention* (Douglas Collection/UA 1973)
Love Child's Afro Cuban Blues Band *Self-titled* (Roulette 1975)
Herbie Mann *Push Push* (Embryo 1971)
Masters of Groove *Masters of Groove Meet Dr. No* (Jazzateria 2001)
Les McCann *Invitation to Openness* (Atlantic 1972)
Freddie McCoy *Funk Drops* (Prestige 1965)
Freddie McCoy *Listen Here* (Prestige 1968)
Galt MacDermot *Shapes of Rhythm* (Kilmarnock 1966)
Galt MacDermot *Hair Pieces* (Verve 1967)
Galt MacDermot *Hamlet* (National 1968) [acetate]
Galt MacDermot *Woman Is Sweeter* (Kilmarnock 1969)
Galt MacDermot *Cotton Comes to Harlem* (UA 1970)
Galt MacDermot *Two Gentlemen of Verona* (Kilmarnock 1970)
Galt MacDermot *The Nucleus* (Kilmarnock 1971)
Galt MacDermot *Ghetto Suite* (Kilmarnock 1972)
Galt MacDermot *Isabel's a Jezebel* (Cast Recording) (UA 1972)
Galt MacDermot *Take this Bread/A Mass in Our Time* (Kilmarnock 1973)
Galt MacDermot *Dude/The Highway Life* (Kilmarnock 1973)
Galt MacDermot *Karl Marx Play* (Kilmarnock 1973)
Galt MacDermot *La Novela* (Kilmarnock 1976)
Galt MacDermot with Pretty Purdie & Bad Bascomb *Live in Nashville* (Kilmarnock 2000)
Galt MacDermot *Up from the Basement* (Kilmarnock 2000)
Galt MacDermot *More from the Basement* (Kilmarnock 2002)
Gary McFarland *America the Beautiful* (Gryphon 1968)
Jimmy McGriff/Groove Holmes *Come Together* (Groove Merchant 1973)
Jimmy McGriff *Supa Cookin'* (Groove Merchant 1973)

Fergus MacRoy *Almost an Hour with Fergus MacRoy* (Kilmarnock 1973)
John Murtaugh *Blues Current* (Polydor 1970)
Oliver Nelson *Swiss Suite* (Flying Dutchman 1971)
David "Fathead" Newman *Bigger & Better* (Atlantic 1968)
David "Fathead" Newman *The Many Facets of David Newman* (Atlantic 1969)
David "Fathead" Newman *Captain Buckles* (Atlantic 1971)
David "Fathead" Newman *This Is the Weapon* (Atlantic 1973)
Frank Owens *Brown'n Serve* (Encounter 1973)
Ralfi Pagán *I Can See* (Fania 1975)
Johnny Pate *Outrageous* (MGM 1970)
Houston Person *Houston Express* (Prestige 1971)
Esther Phillips *From a Whisper to a Scream* (KUDU 1972)
Esther Phillips *Alone Again, Naturally* (KUDU 1972)
Esther Phillips *Performance* (KUDU 1974)
Sonny Phillips *Sure 'Nuff* (Prestige 1969)
Sonny Phillips *Black on Black* (Prestige 1970)
Seldon Powell *Messin' with Seldon Powell* (Encounter 1973)
Profile *Sands of Time* (Encounter 1973)
Pucho & the Latin Soul Brothers *Heat!* (Prestige 1968)
Pucho & the Latin Soul Brothers *Jungle Fire!* (Prestige 1970)
Chuck Rainey Coalition *Self-Titled* (1972)
The Charlie Rouse Band *Cinnamon Flower* (Douglas/Casablanca 1977)
Mongo Santamaria *Stone Soul* (Columbia 1969)
Mongo Santamaria *Workin' on a Groovy Thing* (Columbia 1969)
Mongo Santamaria *Soul Bag* (Columbia 1969)
Mongo Santamaria *Mongo's Way* (Atlantic 1971)
Mongo Santamaria *Afro-Indio* (Vaya 1975)
Mongo Santamaria *Sofrito* (Vaya 1976)
Shirley Scott *Soul Song* (Atlantic 1969)
Shirley Scott *Shirley Scott and the Soul Saxes* (Atlantic 1969)
Stars of Faith *Self-Titled* (Vanguard 1978)

Gil Scott-Heron *Small Talk at 125th & Lenox* (Flying Dutchman 1970)
Gil Scott-Heron *Pieces of a Man* (Flying Dutchman 1971)
Gil Scott-Heron *Free Will* (Flying Dutchman 1972)
Gil Scott-Heron *The Revolution Will Not Be Televised* (Flying Dutchman 1974)
Archie Shepp *For Losers* (Impulse! 1970)
Archie Shepp *Cry of My People* (Impulse! 1973)
Archie Shepp *Kwanza* (Impulse! 1974)
Horace Silver *Silver 'n Brass* (Blue Note 1975)
Nina Simone *Sings the Blues* (RCA 1967)
Jimmy Smith *Respect* (Verve 1967)
Johnny "Hammond" Smith *Here It 'Tis* (Prestige 1970)
Johnny "Hammond" Smith *Soul Talk* (Prestige 1969)
Johnny "Hammond" Smith *Black Feeling!* (Prestige 1969)
Johnny "Hammond" Smith *Wild Horses/Rock Steady* (KUDU 1971)
The Soul Finders *Sweet Soul Music* (Camden 1967)
Dakota Staton *Madame Foo Foo* (Groove Merchant 1972)
Steely Dan *Royal Scam* (ABC 1976)
Steely Dan *Aja* (ABC 1977)
Cat Stevens *Foreigner* (A&M 1973)
Sonny Stitt *Never Can Say Goodbye* (Cadet 1975)
Gabor Szabo *Jazz Raga* (Impulse! 1966)
Leon Thomas *Blues and the Soulful Truth* (RCA 1972)
Leon Thomas *Full Circle* (Flying Dutchman 1973)
Eddie "Cleanhead" Vinson *You Can't Make Love Alone* (Mega 1971)
Grover Washington, Jr. *All the King's Horses* (KUDU 1972)
Marion Williams *Standing Here Wondering Which Way to Go* (Atlantic 1971)
Reuben Wilson & the Cost of Living *Got to Get Your Own* (Cadet 1975)
Jimmy Witherspoon *Spoonful* (Blue Note 1975)
Fritz the Cat (Original Soundtrack Recording) (Fantasy 1972)
HAIR (The Original Cast Recording) (RCA 1967)

In addition to the Wax Poetics staff, Steve Kader and the Sound Library contributed to this pictorial discography.

Pretty Purdie
Soul Drums

Bernard Purdie
Purdie Good!

Pretty Purdie and the Playboys
Stand by Me (Whatcha See Is Whatcha Get)

Bernard Purdie
Soul Is...Pretty Purdie

Bernard Purdie
Shaft

Bernard Purdie
Lialeh OST

Harold Alexander
Sunshine Man

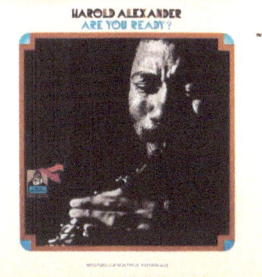
Harold Alexander
Are You Ready?

Gene Ammons
The Boss Is Back!

Louis Armstrong
Louis Armstrong and His Friends

Roy Ayers Ubiquity
Vibrations

Salome Bey
Sings Songs from Dude

Michael Bolotin
Self-Titled

Charlie Brown
Why Is Everybody Always Pickin' on Me?

James Brown
Get on the Good Foot

Oscar Brown, Jr.
Movin' On

Charlie Byrd
The Great Byrd

Charlie Byrd
Aquarius

Buari
Self-Titled

Gary Burton
Good Vibes

Billy Butler
Plays Via Galactica

Joe Cocker
Luxury You Can Afford

Larry Coryell
Coryell

Larry Coryell
Fairyland

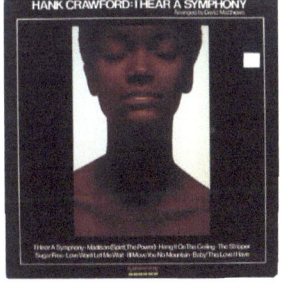
Hank Crawford
I Hear a Symphony

Lou Donaldson
Sweet Lou

Cornell Dupree
Teasin'

Pee Wee Ellis
Home in the Country

Roberta Flack
Quiet Fire

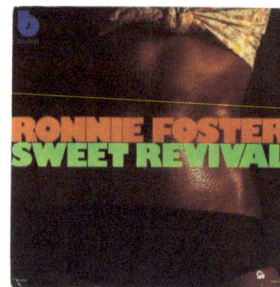
Ronnie Foster
Sweet Revival

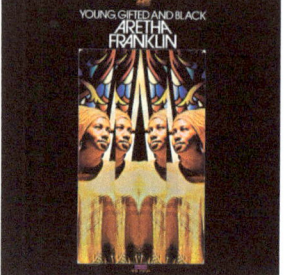
Aretha Franklin
Young, Gifted and Black

Aretha Franklin
Let Me in Your Life

Aretha Franklin
With Everything I Feel in Me

Caesar Frazier
'75

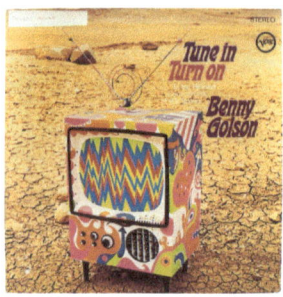
Benny Golson
Tune In, Turn On

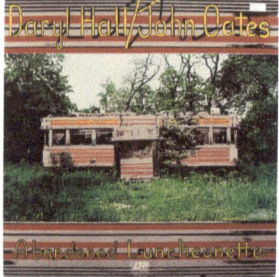
Daryl Hall/John Oates
Abandoned Luncheonette

Herbie Hancock
Fat Albert Rotunda

Ellerine Harding
Ellerine

Eddie Harris & Les McCann
Second Movement

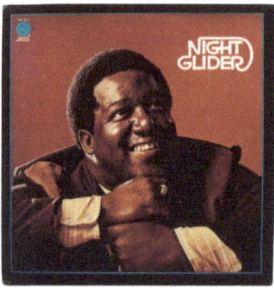
Groove Holmes
Night Glider

Groove Holmes
New Groove

Freddie Hubbard
A Soul Experiment

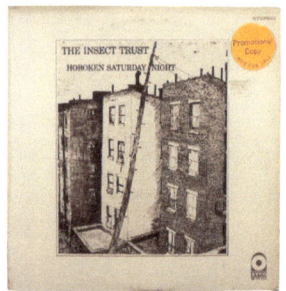
The Insect Trust
Hoboken Saturday Night

Dizzy Gillespie
Cornucopia

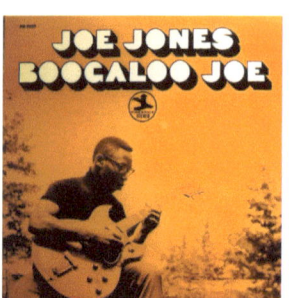
Boogaloo Joe Jones
Boogaloo Joe

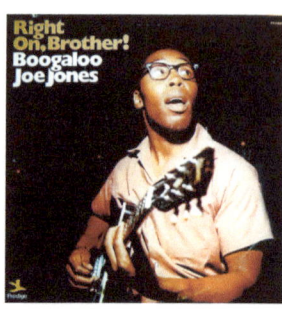
Boogaloo Joe Jones
Right On, Brother!

Boogaloo Joe Jones
No Way!

Boogaloo Joe Jones
What It Is

Quincy Jones
Walking in Space

King Curtis
Live at Fillmore West

King Curtis
Everybody's Talkin'

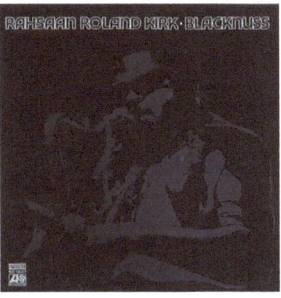
Rahsaan Roland Kirk
Blacknuss

Charles Kynard
Afro-Disiac

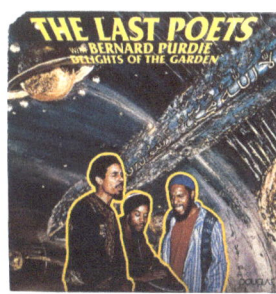
The Last Poets
Delights of the Garden

Lightnin' Rod
Hustler's Convention

Herbie Mann
Push Push

Les McCann
Invitation to Openness

Freddie McCoy
Funk Drops

Galt MacDermot
Shapes of Rhythm

Galt MacDermot
Cotton Comes to Harlem

Galt MacDermot
Two Gentlemen of Verona

Galt MacDermot
The Nucleus

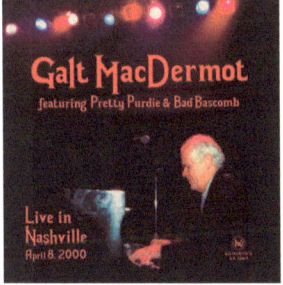
Galt MacDermot
Live in Nashville

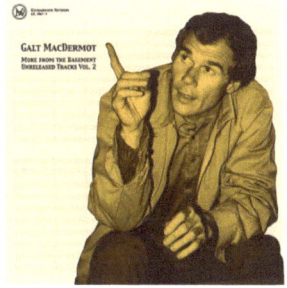
Galt MacDermot
More from the Basement

Jimmy McGriff/Groove Holmes
Come Together

John Murtaugh
Blues Current

Oliver Nelson
Swiss Suite

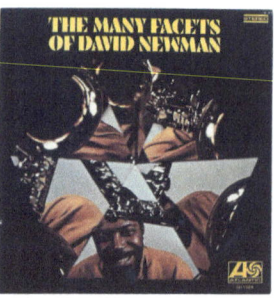
David Newman
The Many Facets of David Newman

David Newman
Captain Buckles

David Newman
This Is the Weapon

Frank Owens
Brown'n Serve

Houston Person
Houston Express

Esther Phillips
From a Whisper to a Scream

Esther Phillips
Alone Again, Naturally

Seldon Powell
Messin' with Seldon Powell

Profile
Sands of Time

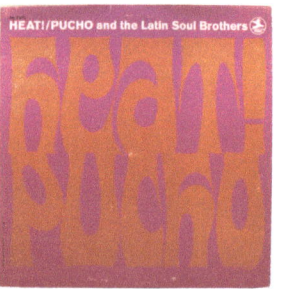
Pucho and the Latin Soul Brothers
Heat!

Pucho and the Latin Soul Brothers
Jungle Fire!

The Chuck Rainey Coalition
Self-Titled

The Charlie Rouse Band
Cinnamon Flower

Mongo Santamaria
Stone Soul

Mongo Santamaria
Workin' on a Groovy Thing

Mongo Santamaria
Soul Bag

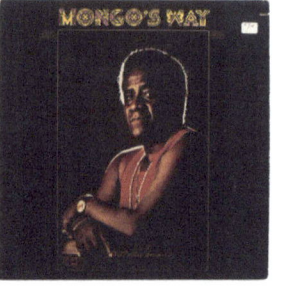
Mongo Santamaria
Mongo's Way

Mongo Santamaria
Afro-Indio

Mongo Santamaria
Sofrito

Shirley Scott
Soul Song

Gil Scott-Heron
Small Talk at 125th and Lenox

Gil Scott-Heron
Pieces of a Man

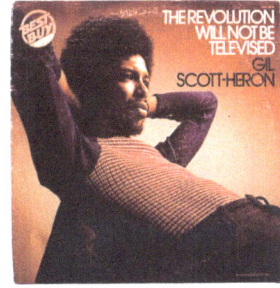
Gil Scott-Heron
The Revolution Will Not Be Televised

Archie Shepp
Kwanza

Horace Silver
Silver 'n Brass

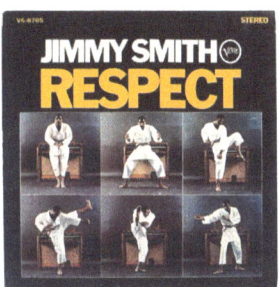
Jimmy Smith
Respect

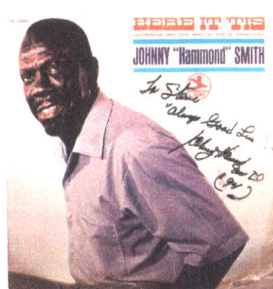
Johnny "Hammond" Smith
Here It 'Tis

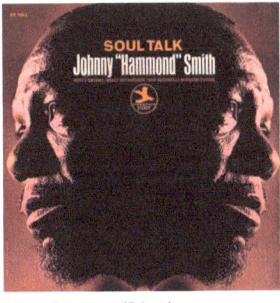
Johnny "Hammond" Smith
Soul Talk

Johnny "Hammond" Smith
Wild Horses/Rock Steady

The Soul Finders
Sweet Soul Music

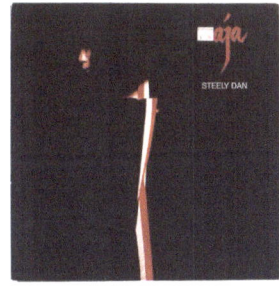
Steely Dan
Aja

Cat Stevens
Foreigner

Gabor Szabo
Jazz Raga

Leon Thomas
Blues and the Soulful Truth

Leon Thomas
Full Circle

Reuben Wilson & the Cost of Living
Got to Get Your Own

Jimmy Witherspoon
Spoonful

Fritz the Cat OST

HAIR (The Original Cast Recording)

"**This is Bob James calling.**" **The voice on the other end of the phone is professional yet friendly. It's the kind of the voice you trust, the kind of voice you'd let sell you term life insurance. It's not, however, the voice of someone you'd think of as an influential figure in hip-hop.**

The button-downed style of Bob James appears to be in stark contrast to that of hip-hop. But then there's the music—funky piano riffs and chunky beats that seemed to have been made with samplers in mind. As an arranger and solo artist at CTI Records in the 1970s, James worked on some of the most sampled records ever made. His version of Paul Simon's "Take Me to the Mardi Gras" was the source of the bells in LL Cool J's "Rock the Bells," as well as Run DMC's "Peter Piper." Then there's "Nautilus," an atmospheric synth vamp that beat junkies can't seem to get enough of. Those two records alone are enough to make James part of hip-hop history. When you factor in the rest of his solo efforts, as well as studio work with the likes of Freddie Hubbard, Hubert Laws, and Grover Washington Jr., among many others, he's nothing short of a legend. James may have the straight-laced look of a high school guidance counsellor, but his razor-sharp sounds have become an irreplaceable part of the hip-hop landscape.

You started out in the background at CTI Records. How did your first CTI solo album come about?

I got to know Creed Taylor [founder of CTI Records] very well. He was making a lot of records and I was one of his main stable arrangers. For a year or two I was going out to Rudy Van Gelder's studio almost on a daily basis. I was working so closely with him that sooner or later the concept came up of me making my own project. His whole plan was to make a lot of albums, so it was not that big a deal for him to go one step further and do one project with me. Frankly, at that time that's all I thought it was going to be—one project that I would have for my memory scrapbooks and to use as a demo to get other jobs. I really didn't have it in my head that a solo career would come out of it. I had a lot of good fortune on that first record.

How did CTI's distinct sound come about?

An awful lot of that credit has to go to Creed Taylor. He had a very specific producer's vision. Because of the fact that he was producing all of the albums on his label, it was inevitable that there would be this stamp. He always used the same engineer, Rudy Van Gelder, so the records had a very distinct sound. Rudy was a brilliant engineer, but a very specific kind of personality. He always had the same kind of drum sound; everything was made in the same studio. That part of it was kind of unique at the time.

Another thing Creed was determined to do was to compete with the pop albums that had a lot bigger budgets. Prior to that an awful lot of the jazz albums were done on such low budgets that the musicians would come in the studio and would have one day to record the whole album, so it was a jam session-type feeling. Creed wanted to have the records sound more competitive with pop, so that it would reach a wider audience, and he started using strings and brass. That was great news for me because my field at the time was doing arrangements for larger orchestral stuff. The fact that Creed wanted that stuff on his records meant a lot of work for me. Since I was doing a lot of arranging on those records, my approach did become part of that CTI sound.

And now that CTI sound has become part of hip-hop.

The whole sampling phenomenon continues to fascinate me. It started out as if it was going to be some short-term, trendy thing, but the whole listening audience has adjusted to it and it becomes part of history, and it's changed the whole course of music.

Why do you think your music has been so popular with DJs and producers?

That's a huge question that I'll probably never know the answer to. Certainly I can't take any credit for initiating the usage of it in that way. It's only been in the last year or so that I've had the opportunity to start thinking about going in the other direction and collaborating with some hip-hop people. Before that, I was playing catch-up to even find out about where my music was being used in all kinds of different ways in recent years. It's almost been shocking to find out that, for whatever reason, my music just became part of the repertoire.

I think, from having talked to a lot of people, that apparently there was a small number of LPs that were in the col-

Bob James Calling
by Jon Azpiri

lections of some of the very early producers of rap albums. The sampling instruments at that time were less sophisticated than they are now, and they would take some of these chunks, looking for rhythmic concepts, and assign them to a note on the keyboard sampling instrument. Once it got in there, it became part of the instrument itself. I think that in some of the cases, they didn't even know who the original artist was. They were looking at it as a button on a keyboard. The fact that I was on some of those buttons made me automatically part of a lot of different records where all I represented was a chunk of sound.

Still, there is something about your music that is very appealing to producers.

We had a lot of pretty simple rhythmic sections too. I was a fan of not filling up every measure with information. Songs like "Nautilus," where the drums and the rhythm section is churning along for at least four bars, became really easy to sample. I was never thinking about it at that time, but part of it is its simplicity. Some music is easier to sample and becomes more neutral underneath rapping or whatever else is going on over top of it.

"Nautilus" has been your most sampled song. What went into making that record?

If you look at it on the LP, it was the last cut on side 2. Back then, you put the things that you thought were going to be least commercial on side 2. "Nautilus" was one of the pieces that no one paid any attention to at all. It was just some little vamp piece that I had come up with. I was experimenting with some early synthesizers at the time—I can't remember what synth it was—and it had this strange sound. Creed Taylor said it reminded him of the sound a submarine makes when it's surfacing. That's how we came up with title "Nautilus."

My thought process on "Nautilus" was not that much different from a lot of the tunes I was working on in that era, coming into the studio with a simple riff that was designed to be a launching pad for improvising. In the early '70s, there was kind of a revolution with some jazz artists that had played with rock groups, and hybrid jazz-rock things happened where the rhythm was not swing any longer. It was more even eighth notes, more rock-influenced drum patterns. It required a different kind of groove, a different kind of soloing, less chords. We were playing bass lines that were repetitive on one chord or two chords. "Nautilus" is an example of that. It's just A minor and the soloing is on a modal scale and you're not soloing on a series of chord changes like the way jazz artists did before when they were improvising on standards.

Another favorite with DJs is "Take Me to the Mardi Gras."

I wanted to make it a party, heavy-Latin thing. I had Ralph MacDonald, who was my favorite percussion player at that time, playing on it. It didn't seem like that much of a big deal at the time we were doing it. Even now, knowing that it's been sampled so much, it's not one of the ones that I take the most pride in having been associated with. Because basically what they sampled was a cowbell introduction that didn't really have anything to do with "Take Me to the Mardi Gras" or my arrangement. It could have been almost anybody. In fact, when I realized that they had to license the use of it and pay a lot of money for it, I was thinking, why didn't they just go in the studio and get a cowbell and play the rhythm part?

Yet there is something very distinct about that record that's hard to duplicate.

It's a particular sound. It's a combination of things. It's Rudy Van Gelder's approach to recording percussion, the way it's mixed, and I had a lot of atmosphere where I was trying to establish that party feeling. All of which ended [up] being appropriate for this other use.

There's a bit of a hip-hop urban legend surrounding one of your records. Biz Markie claims to own a CTI 12-inch single of "Take Me to the Mardi Gras," yet no one seems to have seen it or heard it. Can you confirm or deny that such a record exists?

[*laughs*] I didn't even know the story. I can't confirm it, but it leads me to wonder if it's in the depths of my record collection, in which I have a bunch of promotional items, that Creed would send me, that I never paid any attention to. It didn't occur to me that they would have any value after the LP era was over. All of a sudden, LPs have come back and are coveted.

When did you first become aware that you were being sampled?

A lawyer that knew a friend of mine contacted me and said, "Are you aware that your music is being used for such and such." The record was DJ Jazzy Jeff and the Fresh Prince ["Here We Go Again"]. I went out and got the record and my jaw dropped to the floor. Not only was it a sample of "Westchester Lady," but it was so blatant. I'm listening to this record and thirty seconds of my own recording is playing on its own without them even rapping on it.

On the other hand, I've had artists contact me and ask to license one of my samples, and I listen to a recording and I can't even hear it. I can't hear myself in there anywhere; it's so disguised and layered. They put so many things on top of it that they didn't even have to bother with permission.

You still can be critical of hip-hop and sampling.

There is no correct way of making music. Things change. But for me, making music is a process in which you, as a performer, are playing it from scratch, no pun intended. To have your music depend upon someone else creating it, and then taking chunks out of it and putting it back together again is never going to be quite the same vibe for me as initiating it from the very beginning.

On the other hand, the cut-and-paste aspect of the computer era and the way we think of putting a lot of things together—not just music—and how our minds have adjusted to that, makes it natural to take chunks of things and arrange them in a different order. That phenomenon has changed the way I make music and we'll be seeing that in the new Fourplay project I'm working on.

Have you had the experience where you've heard one of your songs being sampled and you look at your song in a different way?

Sure. That's the best news for me, in the creative sense—when someone brings something new and allows you to see it in a different light. Overall, I have to say that I have to be extremely grateful that, through my music having been so associated with this genre, a lot of young kids end up listening to the original version as a result of its use in this other way.

You recently collaborated with Rob Swift of the the X-Ecutioners.

It was wonderful. He was great, very talented. My friend Milan Simich does some things for a hip-hop label. He was working on a jazz-hip-hop album, taking hip-hop artists and pairing them up with jazz people. He wanted me to work with Rob Swift; he felt [Rob] was one of the strongest rhythmic people in the turntable world and I would enjoy working with him. It was very flattering because Rob was thinking of me as some kind of legend. He was probably surprised that I was still alive.

There is a certain irony in the fact that you've been so influential in hip-hop, yet your image doesn't necessarily fit in to what people think of as hip-hop.

I couldn't be any more removed from that. But that's what was so fun about working with Rob Swift, not that he is the quintessential stereotype of a hip-hop artist, because he isn't. But he lives in a completely different world and he thinks of music in a completely different way. Just bridging the gap and trying to get into the head of at least one of the young people that had grown up in that era was challenging and fun for me.

I guess what I'm saying is that there are stereotypes, but the bottom line is what you sound like. With audio recordings it doesn't make any difference what you look like. It's the sound that comes out.

Jon Azpiri is a freelance writer from Vancouver, Canada. He interviewed Madlib for issue one.

2 BROTHERS WITH BEATS

BY JOE KEILCH – PHOTOS BY BETH FLADUNG

When I asked Mr. Walt how many records they had, the answer was short: "Oh my God." Between a three-story house in Bushwick and a second apartment elsewhere in Brooklyn, they got a lot of fucking records. So many that they can't even count. But Walt says he's the organized one and knows where every record is. I witnessed one argument where Walt accused Evil Dee of not knowing where Public Enemy's "Shut 'Em Down" was and heckled Evil as he tried to find it. He found it.

Two-fifths of the production crew Da Beatminerz, the Brothers Dewgarde—jokesters Mr. Walt and Evil Dee—have made an indelible mark on hip-hop, from Black Moon's *Enta Da Stage* to Smif-n-Wessun's *Dah Shinin'*. And like so many people, their record collection started with vinyl given to them by their parents. But as they began working in record stores, they started taking records much more seriously, not to mention buying a lot more. Mr. Walt worked at Music Factory in Jamaica, Queens for seven years (check ATCQ's "What": "What's Music Factory without Mr. Walt?"). Evil Dee did his record store time at spots like Music Hut in Harlem, Brooklyn's Beat Street, and the Brooklyn Bargain Bazaar, where he learned the mixtape game from DJ Johnny T.

As Walt puts it, "I love shopping for breaks, [for] records. Been doing it twenty years and won't stop." Evil agrees: "Ain't nothing like the feeling of buying a record, coming home and finding a break on it." Walt elaborates, "Got so many records, been doing it so long, now we're record collectors. It's more than just a beat. Buying every Beatles or Pink Floyd record just 'cause you don't have it." I found out that, to the brothers, every record is precious, and no record leaves their collection lightly. During the interview, they argued when divvying up promo records. Walt considered giving me a copy of the new Usher album, and he wanted the one Ghostface 12-inch (with "The Watch" on the b-side) for himself. Both times E wasn't having it; the records stayed in his collection.

CONVENTIONS

They spent years buying the pricey and hard-to-find records at conventions, but ended up very disillusioned. One particular dealer was the straw that broke the camel's back. He had a copy of Bob Azzam's *New Sounds*—with "Rain, Rain, Go Away"—but wouldn't discuss selling it, wouldn't even open his table until Prince Be of PM Dawn was ready. Understandably, they got fed up with the rampant favoritism and the constant reminders of the competition. "At the end of the day," Walt says, "I'm giving you the same green money as PM Dawn, as Kool Herc. Why you gotta act like that?"

Then there were the dealers who jacked up prices when a record was a hit. After Busta Rhymes used it, Seals and Croft records were going for forty bucks. And, as they point out, it's wack from both a collector's and a producer's standpoint. As a collector, there's no reason to pay that much for a common record. As a producer, it doesn't make sense to pay that kind of money for a record that was murdered and is now unusable. In essence, the dealers "saw green; [they] realized, *I can make money off this hip-hop thing.*" Ultimately, the dealers didn't have respect for the music or the record. And now conventions have become circuses, Evil tells me. He realized this when he got his first invitation to a record convention with an MC battle: "Aaaah, it's over."

BUYING TRIPS

They've been all over the world buying vinyl, but trips to New Orleans and Japan are especially memorable. On a trip to New Orleans in the mid-'90s, the routine was this: two vans—one to take Evil Dee, the Boot Camp Clik, Ol' Dirty Bastard, and, occasionally, Kool Keith to do radio interviews, and the other to take Walt, Baby Paul, Posdnous, Pete Rock, and EZ Elpee record shopping. When they'd reunite at the end of the day to hit the clubs, Walt's first words would be, without fail, "Look what I got!"

"Usually Walt buys mad records," Evil Dee says, "but in Japan I bought so much records and *lost* so much records." A box of vinyl shipped via FedEx got caught up in customs and disappeared. They still lament the loss, but haven't slowed down. They still go out every week in NYC to find new joints. "I got spots I can't tell [Evil] about," Walt says. Evil replies, "He's gonna knock me out and take me there." It seems like for now they are done spending big money around the world and at conventions—it's strictly the dollar bins for the brothers. "If it has a rhythm to it and we can mess with it, that's it," they say.

EQUIPMENT

It's well known that Da Beatminerz's studio of choice is the world-renowned—and real fucking grungy—D&D Studio. But, they've also always had a studio in the house, the aptly named Dewgarde Crib of Hits. In 1989 or '90, it began with a little 4-track studio. Before upgrading to a high-speed duplicator, they'd also added a six-foot high stack of tape decks to keep Evil Dee's mixtape production rolling. Then, along with the money from Nervous, came some serious equipment. Now, the back half of the bottom floor of their Bushwick home is filled with turntables and a mixer, an SP 1200, an MPC 2000, an Akai S950, a Roland Juno 106, a Roland digital recording system, a mixing board, and a lot of records. Mr. Walt also has an MPC 3000, an SP, three Akai S900s, an S1000, several mixing boards, and a Juno 106 at his apartment—along with a lot more records. The S950 and the SP are the workhorses, they tell me, while the MPC is mostly used for pitch bending, sampling voices, and stereo sampling.

They've talked about making the kitchen in the Crib of Hits smaller and putting in a vocal booth, but, as Walt puts it, "Mom won't allow it." They do all their pre-production work at the house before going to D&D and are increasingly mixing down more in-house. Evil claims he's the "technical Beatminer," to which Walt responds, "equipment, *shwipment*." Evil then quips, "Walt doesn't make beats no more. Plays a funky trombone."

RESPECT

As hard as it is to believe, these cats had to earn their respect within the beat community. But even as far back as "Who Got Da Props?" they were getting theirs. Evil remembers getting props from Pete Rock because P.R. had always wanted to flip the Ronnie Laws record but could never make it work. Obviously, that's a big compliment. "Then they found out Walt was my brother," Evil

As Walt puts it, "Diamond was the type of cat who'd try to run game on you to see if you knew what you were doing." They ran into each other one time and Diamond asked Walt if he used so-and-so—naming the wrong artist—for the "Bucktown" drums. To which he responded, "Diamond, it's good you're testing, but, c'mon, this is *me*." They know they had to be initiated into the beat community, but Walt has to wonder, "Why can't we just [have bought] the record?"—instead of being accused of stealing the drums.

SAMPLES

But they had the records. "I had all the DJ records," Evil says, "and Walt had all the beats. I had my little beats but nothing extravagant.…You open up Walt's door, you hear *aaaahhhh* [the sound of the perfect beat calling]. I told everybody this, too. I would go beatdigging in my brother's room and find stuff and loop it up. Then Walt comes home [and I'd say], 'Look what I made.' That whole Black Moon/Smif-n-Wessun, that's me digging in Walt's stuff."

For the brothers, making beats has increasingly become a race. "You're just racing to see who's gonna come out with it first," Walt says. "Hoping that the other person's sample isn't gonna be so big that you can't ever touch that sample again. Something like 'I Know You Got Soul' or 'Put Your Hands Where My Eyes Can See'? C'mon, it's over!" He recently got beat to the finish line. He was working on a Black Moon song for a *High Times* album and was chopping up the same Toni Braxton sample that ended up in Redman and Method Man's "Part Two." Walt was "shanghaied again. It was like someone was looking in my window like, 'Oh, Toni Braxton.' Yo, it was so uncanny. No fucking way. I couldn't believe it. Just coincidence. In this game, if you've got an idea, hurry up with it."

Evil mentions, "I get shanghaied for beats by my own brother." ("That's right," Walt interrupts.) "I'll be looping something up," Evil continues, "and the record will disappear. [*laughter*] And Walt'll be like, 'Wanna hear this new beat?' That's the record! '*No it ain't!*'"

PRODUCTION

These cats got tricks when it comes to making beats. Somewhere in all our collections we've got a record that looks like someone ice-skated on it. When Walt's sampling something that is too clean (didn't think there was such a thing, did you?), he grabs an ice-rink record and samples surface noise, clicks, and fuzz to lay over top the too-clean sample. But their main trick, Walt says, is simply to "listen to the whole record. That's when you find the shit you missed." Evil agrees: "I buy records just to listen to it. The beat for 'Bentleys and Bitches'—I bought that record to listen to 'cause I like Norman Whitfield as a producer."

says. "Ohhh, my whole secret was revealed. Everybody was like, 'This cat knows his beats'…'Mr. Walt from Music Factory is your brother?' It was out the bag."

One memorable entrance exam to becoming part of the beat community came when Diamond tested Walt on the drums that they had used for "Bucktown." The reputation-ruining rumor circulating at the time was that they'd stolen them from one of two places and didn't actually own the record. The first possible source was Apache's "Hey Girl"—Large Professor had used the same drums and left them open. And the second was Da Beatminerz's remixing of a Tribe Called Quest song that had the same drums. Q-Tip accused Walt of stealing the drums off their two-inch reel. And, because sampling from hip-hop records was considered a mortal sin, the beat heads were bugging.

DJ PREMIER

Both admit that DJ Premier catches them sleeping on things in their own collection. "Preem comes to our house," Walt says, "and looks through records. 'Oh, this is what I used for such and such.' I'm like, 'I had this record and didn't use it before you did? *Aaaahhh!*'"

"I think the funniest record Preem used," Evil remembers, "that he pulled out on me—and I looked at him like, *you asshole*—was the Les McCann for '10 Crack Commandments.'" "I hate that!" Walt yells. "Asshole," Evil jokes.

KEYBOARDS

When we discussed the current trend of keyboard-driven hip-hop, Mr. Walt and Evil Dee gave props to the Neptunes for creating their own sound. And although Walt knows how to play, they only use keyboards to enhance sampled bass lines. "I can't turn my back on [sampling]," Walt says. "It's gotta have a sample in it. Regardless of what I tell [people buying my beats], it's gotta have one. I can't turn my back on that type of music.…Even though what we sample isn't original…it [becomes] original 'cause we take it and flip it into something else. But there's no originality if you're using the same sounds as Swizz Beatz."

THE FUTURE

Da Beatminerz have had the mixed fortune of being involved with two of the most well-known record labels in the rap game: Nervous and Rawkus. They've since moved on—a little jaded but a lot wiser—and, even without the backing of an established record label, aren't slowing down. They've got two beats on Naughty By Nature's new album and three on Smif-n-Wessun's upcoming long player. They're working on a new Black Moon album and a remix for Dilated Peoples. And Evil Dee has a remix mixtape in the works. They're also going to resuscitate Pandemonium Wrekordz, the label that put out Finsta's "Crush" 12-inch and the Shades of Brooklyn 12-inches. They're also out buying beats every week and DJing at Bar XVI in Manhattan every Thursday night. But, most importantly, they're chilling with their family (Moms lives upstairs from E's apartment and the studio and Walt lives with his son and girlfriend), keeping heads bobbing, and keeping people around them laughing. ⬤

Joe Keilch (aka DJ Eleven) is a writer and DJ living in Brooklyn, New York. He interviewed Rob Corrigan of the Sound Library for issue one.

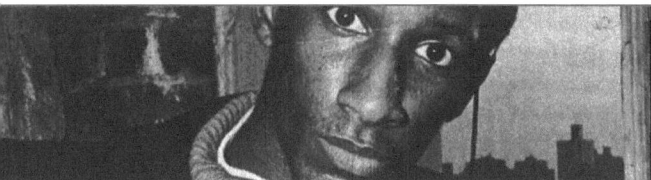

First Phase
by Steven Hager
from *East Village Eye*
November 1982

reprinted with permission

"I met Phase in 1973, shortly after I founded United Graffiti Artists. The first half of graffiti was primarily execution: quantity, bravado, risks, etc., but the second half was based on style. I'd heard about a writer named Phase 2 who had so many styles that he was giving them out to other writers. I knew he was the major influence in the Bronx, so I invited him to UGA. When he came in the door, it was obvious I was dealing with an amazing creative source. His energy was all over the place. His body was alive; the place was bopping. What do I think of Phase today? I think he's a genius. I think he's the godfather of style."

–Hugo Martinez, Oct. 1982

Exactly ten years ago, the first organized attempt to market subway graffiti as art began when Hugo Martinez invited twelve writers to spray-paint a 10 × 40 foot paper-covered wall at City College. Martinez's efforts to legitimize graffiti eventually fizzled and most people expected the "fad" to fizzle along with it.

It didn't happen. Graffiti went back underground, periodically surfacing at various galleries and alternative spaces around New York. Recently, graffiti has been invigorated by its connection with the hip-hop music scene. It has been hyped in *Art in America*, *Art Forum*, *Arts Magazine*, and *Art News*. It has been widely imitated by art students. In fact, graffiti seems destined to take its rightful place in art history.

But where is this place?

Before anyone will determine the answer, both factions of the current graffiti controversy will have to cool down and take a close look at what is covering the walls and subway trains of this city. At this point, blanket acceptance is no more helpful than blanket condemnation. There can be no doubt that most graffiti being done today is boring and poorly executed. But the same could be said for most art. The only notable difference is that bad artists have difficulty foisting their sensibility on an unreceptive audience, while bad graffiti writers find it relatively easy. The true promise and potential of graffiti has always resided in the work of a small core of master writers. Remove the contribution of these few writers and one is left with an exciting, daredevil sport—but no art to speak of. And no other single writer has contributed more to the history of graffiti as art than Phase 2, who continues to live an existence of quiet anonymity, despite his legendary status within the subculture.

☙

They say it started in 1969. Contrary to popular belief, the first graffiti writers claim they did not start marking up the city in an attempt to make themselves famous. They wrote because it was fun. At first, no one paid much attention to them. It was just a secret little hobby shared by a small band of non-conformists. The introduction of the magic marker in the late '60s had provided the necessary technology; the will had been around since time immemorial.

In the summer of 1971, the *New York Times* inadvertently created a mini-boom in graffiti when it sent a reporter to find out the mysterious identity of "Taki 183." The reporter tracked down a likeable seventeen-year-old who said: "You don't do it for the girls. They don't seem to care. You do it for yourself." The article appeared on July 21, and Taki was enshrined forever in the graffiti hall of fame. Who knows how many kids went out the next day and bought magic markers as a result of that story?

Solo graffiti (as distinct from gang graffiti) probably started on the Upper West Side, but it wasn't until the trend moved in to the South Bronx that its full potential was realized. By 1971, the graffiti writer was well on his way to becoming the new urban hipster: part outlaw, part artist, part daredevil—it was a synthesis that proved irresistible.

Sly II was the first writer on 163rd Street in the Bronx. He was quickly followed by Lee 163, who developed a uniquely stylized signature, stacking and fusing the letters in his name like a corporate logo. Lee began writing in March 1971. In October, his friend Phase 2 appeared. "Phase had

The evolution of the Phase 2 tag from 1971 to 1974

a positive reaction to my graffiti," says Lee. "But he wasn't going to start writing just because I was. He's always had his own mind. He waited until he was ready."

"The previous year we'd given this party," explains Phase. "We were getting ready to give another party and I said, 'We'll call this one phase two.' It was like I discovered something, like it was destiny. I don't know why, but I was stuck on the name. It had meaning for me."

Phase worked his way into the subculture slowly. It wasn't until he visited the West Side and saw Cay 161's work that he became obsessed with "bombing." "Cay was a fucking madman," he says. "When I saw what he was doing, I said, 'This is the way it's supposed to be done. I'm going back up to the Bronx and tear shit up.' I became a madman 'cause I was kinda sick too. People write for different reasons, but there's basically two types. Either you're in or you're out. Either you're dedicated or you're not. Graffiti has meaning for me, it holds strength. It's not some bullshit. I was out there because I wanted to bomb, man! Another ten years from now, the guys that are really dedicated will still be saying, 'Yeah, I remember when we used to ride the trains.'"

At the time, Phase was tall, skinny, and almost always wore a hat jauntily perched on his head. A French cap made by Flechet was his favorite. He projected an almost explosive sense of urgency; his occasional stuttering heightening the impression his physical being was struggling to keep pace with a galloping imagination. While talking, he frequently twisted and clenched his fingers, as if creating a pattern for some bizarre new lettering style. He was outgoing and seemed to know everyone in the Bronx. "You couldn't walk down the street with him without his saying hello to a dozen people," says one friend. Few people, however, knew Phase was a writer.

"I tried to keep a low profile," he says. "For quite a while nobody knew I was Phase 2. I told my friends not to tell anyone. That was the fun of it. You could sit around and people would say, 'Damn, you know who I want to meet? Phase 2.' And I'd be sitting right next to them."

In 1973, Super Kool 223 revolutionized graffiti by spraying large outlines of his signatures on the outside of trains, outlines that were painstakingly filled in with paint. "Everybody was damn negative about it at first," says Phase. "Even I thought the shit was crazy. It took a whole can of paint! With one can you could write your name so many damn times. But then everybody picked up on it. I remember seeing some block letters by Sentry 120. That's when I came out with my softie letters. People started calling it the bubble style."

The giant signatures became known as "masterpieces" and it suddenly became necessary to steal a lot of paint in order to execute them.

"Super Kool and his girlfriend were the first to rack up huge quantities," says Phase. "He was always dressed very dapper. He didn't look the type. But stealing went along with the graffiti shit. I didn't get into it, but a lot of guys did. Not just paint, but leather coats, stereos. One time I led about twenty guys into a store. We went straight to the paint. Something came over me. I slapped all the cans off the shelf. It was crazy. There was so much confusion. Guys were screaming. The salesman tried to keep us in the store. Guys had to throw blows to get out. The mounted police

came. We ran around the corner and had four cans of paint between twenty guys. That wasn't the way to do it."

In October of 1972, Hugo Martinez, a sociology student at City College, founded United Graffiti Artist (UGA), a quasi-democratic organization designed to take master writers off the street and provide them with a more professional environment. "At first the group was all Puerto Rican except for one Greek," says Martinez. "Three or four members did not want to accept Blacks. I knew the Black writers from the Bronx represented the birth of the masterpiece, so I tried to manipulate votes and put pressure on certain individuals to bring them into the group."

Getting Up: Subway Graffiti in New York (a book by Craig Castleman published last month) characterizes Martinez as a racist who was very reluctant to allow Blacks into UGA. Martinez, who was not interviewed for the book, hotly denies the allegation.

"The first graffiti writers were members of gangs," he says. "I was dealing with a few gang members whose biggest enemy was the Bronx. I couldn't be overt about what I was doing."

One thing is certain: there was a tremendous amount of racial tension at UGA, which was unusual since most writers at the time respected each other regardless of color. "I think he favored the Puerto Ricans," says Lee 163, "Sometimes he would hold meetings with them and we wouldn't find out until later."

The tension eventually flared into a full-scale rumble at UGA headquarters on Jumel Place at 168th Street. UGA member Henry 161 showed up one day accompanied by five or six members of the Young Galaxies, a local street gang. They immediately began trashing the studio. "I got hit in the head with a stick," says Phase. "Hugo did too. It was fucking crazy. Henry got kicked out of the group. I later found out certain writers felt threatened by us."

There were other problems, like the controversy between Snake 1 and Snake 131. Snake 131 was considered to be the original Snake and to prove it, he started writing "Snake 1-131." It was too much for Snake 1 to bear. He went to Snake 131's house armed with a revolver. "It wasn't like they didn't like each other," says Phase. "They were both members of the group. Snake 1 just said: 'Drop the fucking 1,' and left." Fortunately, Snake 131 dropped it.

Why did the writers take their efforts so seriously? "We were devoted 'cause it belonged to us," says Phase. "It was ours. Nobody could take it away from us."

In the three years of UGA's existence, several exhibitions were held. Phase 2 and AMRL (also known as Bama) established themselves as the most talented painters. Both sold canvases in the $2,000 price range. Phase was the major stylistic innovator; AMRL a superb colorist.

According to their own press releases, UGA members had stopped writing on trains. This was actually a publicity gimmick intended to smooth over relations with the outside world. Phase *had* slowed down on hitting trains, but his concepts always found their way to the yards, primarily through Riff 170. "They fed off each other," says Martinez. "They were like Lennon and McCartney. They were a synthesis of style and execution. Riff had a photographic memory. They say he had a shutter in his eye. Phase got his source from inside. He might be influenced by other things, but you never really know where he gets his ideas. How he conceptualizes things is beyond me."

Phase was continually altering his lettering style. He would fuse letters, extend them, twist them, elongate them. The letters got increasingly ornate and experimental. The style was extremely popular with other writers in the Bronx and soon became a dominant force in graffiti. A writer named Tracy 168 picked it up and began calling it "wild style."

Meanwhile, Phase and AMRL accepted scholarships from Pratt, where they studied illustration and commercial art. Phase lasted three years before dropping out. "I got a sense of how to execute at Pratt," he says. "The work there was very sophisticated. It didn't really influence the direction of my work, but I was aware of the quality of what they were doing. I left because there were too many problems, and too much other shit was going on."

The hip-hop scene was growing and Phase had become an integral part of it. His dancing style had always been wild and innovative—just like his art—and Phase was a pioneer of break dancing. He began creating flyers for an old friend named Kool DJ Herc, as well as for a new up-and-coming DJ named Grandmaster Flash. (The man most responsible for the creation of hip-hop music, Kool Herc also wrote graffiti in the early '70s before becoming a DJ. "Yeah, graffiti started it all," admits Herc.)

"I don't mean to brag," says Phase, "but I knew how to innovate those flyers. I knew how to advertise. Me, Sisco Kid, Buddy Esquire, Riley, Danny T., we helped push those rappers. We hyped them with some really vicious flyers. I think the flyers helped build hip-hop. Herc set the pace for the scene but the first real rapping I remember was Cowboy. Flash would play "Bongo Rock" [note: the real title is "Apache" by the Incredible Bongo Band] and Cowboy would say: "To the rock, rock, rock. South side… make money. Easy side …make money.' It sounded *so* bad. The impact was there. It made sense and added so much to the music."

Never one to imitate another's style, Phase soon developed the "crooning rap," a vocal style that combined rap lyrics with real singing. "About three years ago I saw him win a talent show at the Ecstasy Garage," says Kool Herc. "I

GRAFFITI: the formative years, 1969–74, as recalled by Phase 2

JULIO 204
first to combine name with street number

COCO 144
first 3-dimensional

TAKI 183
first to tag train stations

LEE 163
first completely stylized signature

BABY FACE 86
first crown

SUPER KOOL 223
first to fill-in outline (masterpiece); first to "rack up" paint; first top-to-bottom; first whole car

didn't even know he could sing. He's got a good voice. He's just waiting for his big break."

That break may have arrived: A French record company has recently asked Phase to record a single for them. If it happens, it can't be soon enough for Phase, who often seems desperate to escape the South Bronx.

"It has changed like crazy," he says. "You don't even want to be here anymore. That's how I feel. The shit started with the blackout in '77. That just totaled the whole damn neighborhood. People ransacked the stores and the businesses never came up out of it. It was the start of something bad. A person with some kind of feelings doesn't belong here anymore. It seems like evil prevails. Everybody has a fucked up attitude. I want to get out, move to some corner of the world where they only kill one person a year. I don't belong in this shit. Everything is a fucking gimmick these days. Everybody is a phony. I respect making money only when people see a purpose for what they're doing. So many writers are thinking out of synch, crossing out each other's names. Before, we always had respect. You might hate a guy's guts, thought he was a sucker, but still said, *Damn, he sure can paint*. A lot of these guys today don't realize what we went through. We went from one stage to the next at random. The skeleton of graffiti has been out since '76. All the shit was laid down. I think what they're doing today is fucking crazy. Too much marking on the insides. It looks pathetic."

It seems strange that despite his privileged status in graffiti history, Phase 2 has not had a gallery show in over six years. This oversight is primarily due to the fact that he has never pushed his work. He still draws continuously, however, and his latest sketches represent the cutting edge of the new "alien machine" style. "I relate to unearthly things," he says. "You might think it's crazy, but I think I had a previous life in Egypt. That's where I get a lot of my ideas." ⊙

Author of Hip Hop: The Illustrated History of Break Dancing, Rap Music, and Graffiti *(1984),* Art After Midnight: The East Village Scene *(1986), and* Adventures in the Counterculture, STEVEN HAGER *is now editor-in-chief of* High Times.

PHASE 2

first window-down whole car; first writer with multi-styles; first drips; first clouds; first cut-up letters; first bubble-style letters; first abstract clouds; first hump letters; first transparent letters; first arrows; first loops; first extension bars; first faces as letters

JAPAN

first whole train (10 cars)

TRACY 168

first to innovate characters; first tiger stripes; invented term "wild style" to describe lettering first created by Phase 2

PISTOL

first 3-dimensional masterpiece

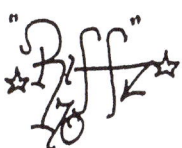

RIFF 170

first two-color pieces; first color concepts; first character whole cars; first puzzle designs; first marshmallow letters; first cracked letters

NORTH COAST HIP-HOP: STEP INTO A WORLD
An allegory in four parts

by Daniel Gray-Kontar
illustration by Andrew Robinson

dj PRIME
digin in the cr...

I am/The Seer/galactic griot/funk historian/I resuscitate verbs/ unheard/felt through the galaxy/inhale rhythm/life/write it down/ever watching/after a millennium/you learn to notice/ which events across the universe/are worthy of note/even the omnipotent/must choose moments to study/closest/this brings Me to/My current entry.

on the young planet/earth/there is a tremor/soul stirring movement/worth The Seer's/sight. a corner of the globe/a land named amerigos/center of the seventh of earth's seven worlds/those who dwell in this land/call this small corner/the northern coast/amongst what are called/the great lakes/a place where aquarian fluidity/meets geminian communication.

here/a small band of/superhuman creators/who know not their extra-sensory/superhuman powers/create new realms/ fusing the past and future/a neo-present/they have no knowledge of the strength of their words/rhythms/in the realm of the unseen/yet the tremors they make/shake the universe/enough to evoke the curiosity of/The One/who has felt seven trillion tremors/arousing/yet/these rhythms/are different/come along only once/in/1,000 lifetimes.

ONE:

The Seer peers inside the living room of the MC Jermaine Sands, whose code name is J. Sands. Sands is one-half of the rap duo called the Lone Catalysts. Without his knowledge, Sands, based in Pittsburgh, PA, commands the superhuman ability to communicate his thoughts across the planet, with the help of a cowrie shell ring given to him by a wise sage. With his words, Sands communicates a rare quality on earth known as "realness." His poetic message reaches only those listeners who know how to "hear." The Seer watches as Sands rehearses freshly written lyrics inside his living room. As Sands spits his verse, his superpower (aura) spreads throughout the universe.

> J. SANDS: "I claim thrones/like Persian kings/my urban theme/is to keep my culture pure/and untampered/like virgin queens."

The Seer, hearing Sands's lyrics, locks into his mind, and spits the rest of the verse in unison along with him. Sands's cowrie shell ring begins to glow.

> THE SEER: *once again/the tremor begins.*

> J. SANDS and THE SEER: I'm like the friendliest/love and peace to everyone/same thing back to me/that beef shit is wack to me/because actually/I found out the facts to be/that if you have beef it's to the death, naturally…

> J. SANDS: [*feeling as though he's not alone*] Damn. What the fuck?

The telephone rings. J. Sands snaps out of his strange feeling to answer it. On the other end of the line is Sands's partner in the Lone Catalysts, Jason Rawls—code name J. Rawls. Rawls also has super powers, which he has no knowledge of: the ability to stir spirits through his manipulation of circular discs called "records." Whenever Rawls places a record on a machine called a "turntable," the spirits of past musicians are stirred. Rawls has the uncanny ability to fuse the past with the present to create neo-rhythms. Whenever Rawls creates, he absorbs the super powers of the musicians who came before him, whose work he has fused. Rawls, who is based in Columbus, OH, is about 300 miles from J. Sands.

[*on the telephone*]

> J. RAWLS: 'Sup man? I felt you.
> J. SANDS: Just wrote this new rhyme, son.
> J. RAWLS: That's what's up. I just heard from Mazi, yo.
> J. SANDS: Word? Mazi from Cleveland?
> J. RAWLS: Yeah. He found that breakbeat record I was looking for.
> J. SANDS: Which one?
> J. RAWLS: The Hot Chocolate breakbeat.
> J. SANDS: Hot Chocolate?
> J. RAWLS: Yeah. Some old soul/funk cats from Cleveland. Back in the '70s.
> J. SANDS: Never heard of them cats.
> J. RAWLS: Ain't nobody ever heard of them. But it's hot shit. You gotta spit on this one jawn on there, man. It's killin 'em.
> J. SANDS: Tell me when.
> J. RAWLS: Soon as you get here.
> J. SANDS: This weekend?
> J. RAWLS: A'ight.

I am The Seer/it/begins/the birth of a new rhythm/world/so be it.

TWO:

Toby Brazwell, code name Heiku, sits in the living room of his apartment in Columbus, OH. Heiku is one-half of another superhero duo called Edotkom. With his beats, he has the ability to open gateways into the future. Meanwhile, his partner in Edot, Brandon Terry has a similar power. Code named Siege, the Cleveland-based MC wields the power to open gateways into the past. When the two link together, they have the ability to bring both worlds—past and future—into the present. Like J. Sands and J. Rawls, both are unaware of the powers they control in the realm of the unseen.

Heiku, who has just finished writing, closes his book of rhymes and walks over to his personal computer. After turning it on, he logs onto the Internet and sends a copy of new rhymes to Siege.

> HEIKU WRITES: You feeling these? Just some shit I wrote. Was thinking about calling it "IMMUNIZATION."

…Packin' a mack in the back of an Ac/practically back slapping ya with the Rogaine to get it back/cuz the Black/rap attack/tackling mikes and hack 'em/and praised by veteran thugs/MCs yelling at the infallible/battle rappable/canibal/hannibal/lector/lecture trinity/get in thee/send the enemy/back to black boards/creativity/contest the unrest/just surrounded by calamity.

> SIEGE WRITES: Hot shit. I think I got rhymes to match. "IMMUNIZATION" is fresh.
> HEIKU WRITES: Word. Sending you a beat for it now.
> SIEGE WRITES: A'ight. I'll listen to it, and construct some other shit that might fit too. When you wanna put it down?
> HEIKU WRITES: What's up with Saturday?
> SIEGE WRITES: Cool.

I am The Seer/the process is almost complete/only synchronicity is needed to open a new realm of verbal rhythm/if the lone catalysts stir the spirits of the past/communicating their words to the mass of listeners who can hear/it will be good/should edotkom open the realms of the past and future/it will complete the birth of a new sound/where neo-rhythms will be born/imagine/a conversation between past and future/blast throughout the galaxy/an underground theme for the ages/it will be good.

THREE:

J. Sands is in J. Rawls's at-home recording studio. Lining the walls of the studio are more than 5,000 records. Rawls pulls one of the records from the stacks as Sands goes over his rhimes. The record is a copy of "So Ruff, So Tuff" by Roger Troutman, which he places on the turntable. Rawls listens to the record, and soon, a conversation begins in his mind. The rhythm guitar from the track transforms into the repetitive phrase: "Soul is life. Soul is life." The drum track from the record also morphs into another phrase: "God's love. God's love." As Rawls's mind settles into these phrases, the music communicates with him further. Soon, the music is no longer music. It becomes the voice of the deceased Roger Troutman himself, a native of Dayton, Ohio.

see brother? listen. "soul is life." "God's love." that's what that record was really talking about, man. hear it? we couldn't communicate in the same way that you brothers can now, man, do you know how much power is in the word and the rhythm combined? the power holders/the unseen ones/they always knew the power of nommo. *they cut our power to speak so that our tongues could not spread positive messages. Today, they have given you the power to use your tongues/but they cut you off from the rhythm. So, now, you all have the power to speak, but you don't listen. so, to fight the overspeech, you gotta add groove to it. but it gotta be the right rhythms, brother. you gotta do it. becuz soul is life, man. and life is nothing but the love of God manifesting in everything surrounded by you. you are one of the few to get this communication. use it. speak it. i give you my power to bring forth* ashe *through rhythm. speak with your hands. speak, brother. speak. soul is life. soul is life. God's love. God's love.*

The communication ends, and the groove returns to its normal state. J. Rawls samples from a piece of the rhythm guitar. He also cuts a small piece of the drum track, adding both samples to the main loop from the Hot Chocolate album. To the world, the two loops will sound like another drum and guitar loop. To those that can hear, they will feel the true meaning. When Rawls finishes the rough version, J. Sands steps into the recording booth. He puts on the headphones and gets ready to add vocals to the track.

The Seer: *the manifestation is nearly completed/it is/an exciting/time.*

FOUR:

As the Lone Catalysts are in their Columbus studio working on their new project, Heiku and Siege are at Siege's Cleveland apartment recording "Immunization."

Siege: From the actual to the physical/mental to metaphysical/visual to the spiritual/I conquer all dimensions/siege, the non-visible/bonds a little pitiful/typical lyricals?/I can crush you with a syllable…

J. Sands: Number one on the list/no need to front on this shit/it's a blessing I don't have to think with the gun on the hip/got 'nuff ice in the freezer/don't need none on the wrist/just trees and mo' Henny/that's how I come in this bitch

Suddenly, a bright light appears simultaneously in Columbus and Cleveland.

Heiku: What the…?

J. Sands: Yo, Jay. What's going on, man?

The Seer: *it begins/a new spirit world/born.*

From the light emerge visions of groups from the past and future of North Coast music. From the Cleveland studio, groups from the past climb out of narrow cipher, their essential forms spitting into the air like rockets of light. Roger Troutman, the Ohio Players, RAMP, the Dazz Band, Sounds of Unity and Love (S.O.U.L.), Lou Ragland, and countless others all appear from the light in Cleveland. Meanwhile, from the light in Columbus, in similar fashion, the Five Deez, the Diggin' in the Crates Crew, DJ Prime, Homeskilit, and the Animal Crackers emerge from the light. Just as quickly as it appears, the light disappears.

To all of the members involved, it appears to be a brief malfunction to their sound equipment. They continue.

I am The Seer/it is unleashed/the past and future of rhythm/verse/a new spiritual realm/unseen/felt/the universe will never be the same/here/where the past/present/and future/meet/a new legacy/may the new rhythm spawn a new listener/a soul revolution/of the first order/may the wielders of this revolution/power/never know of their true might/keep their strength pure/untainted/free/so be it.

●

Daniel Gray-Kontar *is a poet and journalist from Cleveland, Ohio. He is a staff writer and assistant music editor for the* Cleveland Free Times, *Ohio's largest alternative news and entertainment weekly.*

Andrew Robinson *is the creator of* Dusty Stax, *and has worked in comics for the past eight years. He currently lives in Pasadena, CA, and is very happy.*

Love and Hate:

by Oliver Wang – photos by Jessica Miller

Opened in 1989, San Francisco's Groove Merchant is arguably the oldest record store in the United States specializing in rare soul, jazz, Latin, and other funky thangs. Nestled away in SF's relaxed, hip Lower Haight neighborhood, the store remains the premier rare groove shop this side of the Mississippi. The brainchild of the husband/wife team of Mike and Jody McFadden, the store was part of an integrated mini-empire of musical outposts, including their successful labels—Ubiquity (new electronic), Luv n' Haight (reissue soul/funk/jazz), and CuBop (Afro-Latin). Since 1994, though, "Cool" Chris Veltri has become the store's most visible presence, having started as an employee for two years, then a manager for two, and since 1998, Groove Merchant's sole owner. He also runs, along with DJ Vinnie Esparza, two labels: DisJoint (new music) and ReJoint (reissues). Wax Poetics's Oliver Wang recently spoke to Mike McFadden and Cool Chris to chart the past, present, and future of Groove Merchant.

Wax Poetics: Mike, when you started the store in 1989, was there anything else like it that you knew of?

Mike McFadden: As far as I know, it was the only store. I had been to LA, New York, Chicago…I didn't know any store that had specialized just in [rare groove]. It was modeled after a London store—even though we had never been in London. We just based it on what we heard of them.

Did you have a clear idea of what you wanted the store to be and who it would serve?

MM: It wasn't well thought out—all we wanted to do is be surrounded by the music we liked and be able to make enough money to pay the rent. We were just really into rare groove, and found a way to work with what we loved.

Given that this was a fairly new concept, did you find much support for the idea initially?

MM: There were a few naysayers that we had to ignore, but we had guys from England, Japan, and Europe coming in. It grew into enough of a business.

What were you into and how did that influence how you stocked the store?

MM: In my early twenties, we had started getting into the underground club business. It might be anything from old JB's cuts, to hip-hop, to what they called acid house, to "Spill the Wine" by Eric Burdon, to Iggy Pop. It was just an eclectic mix. Once I started listening to stuff like the JB's, I got hooked and started buying any records that looked to be similar. A lot of the rare grooves that we sold out of Groove Merchant were things we had discovered just by buying records. For example, no one had been buying the 24-Carat Black record, and then we started selling it and people got hip to it.

Chris, what's changed with Groove Merchant over the last ten years?

Chris Veltri: The store hasn't drastically changed. We're still stocking the same stuff that we've stocked since the store opened in '89. The dynamic hasn't changed much. Though when the whole DJ thing got huge a few years back, it brought in people asking for strange things—"intelligent drum and bass"—just a weird clientele, which I immediately tried to drive out of the store.

How much of the current store is reflective of your particular tastes?

CV: I think it could be as specialized as I am, 'cause a lot of the stuff in the store is handpicked. There is definitely not a record fairy that comes in and sprinkles those records every week; as much as I'd like that, it just doesn't fucking happen. There's just some things that I really like [to have] in the store, and I really forcefully go after them.

 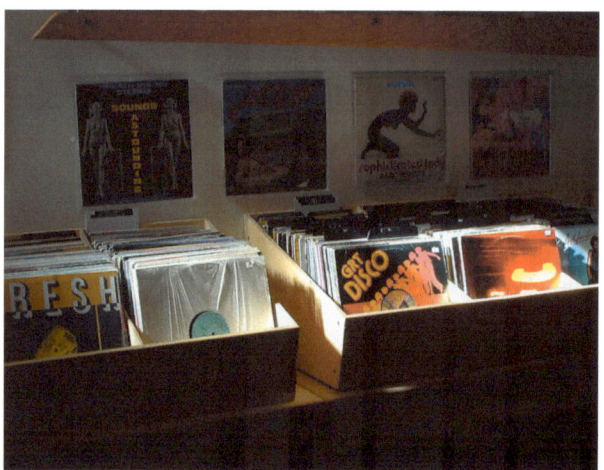 

San Francisco's Groove Merchant

There's some things you can't depend on just coming to you through the door; you just have to really make the calls, find the contacts, and just get in your car and drive.

Is it hard to separate your personal collection from what you sell at the store?

CV: I really have to put the store ahead of my collection. There's certain things on my list that, if they pop up, I mark off my list and I take them home. A lot of records I put out, I don't have and would like to own but (*a*) I need the money, and (*b*) I really do try to keep the store interesting.

Because Groove Merchant is the only real store of its kind out here, do you think it's played an influential role in bringing to light certain rare albums?

CV: I feel like I've discovered a few things. One of the few things I'm fairly certain I've broken recently is this one record that came out of Mexico by Lito Barrientos. I turned up maybe eighteen of them and they went all over the place, a lot of them went to Europe. I kind of think I broke Bwana to an extent 'cause I had a massive amount of copies of it, over one hundred. Mike [McFadden] was one of the early people to really push 24-Carat Black—he had like a hundred sealed copies of that. Same with Nathan Davis's *If*. But who's to say? You can never really say, there's always someone before you.

Now that funk 45s and library records are at their zenith, what do you see on the horizon in terms of digging trends?

CV: I think people will slowly start embracing the '80s, if they haven't already. Brazilian seems to go away, come back stronger, go away, come back even stronger. I think '60s jazz and private issue jazz is going to be one of the next big things. [And] just straight up, hard-to-find soul records. Not that any of these things were ever unpopular. Even Mo' Wax-era 12-inches that people at the time didn't really take for what it is—and now they just ain't out there. I think the 12-inch is really going to take off in the years to come. The indie hip-hop thing is going to go bananas.

I know one of the toughest things you have to deal with is pricing out your records. People just assume that specialty stores mark up their prices just because they know they can get away with it. But break it down—how do you determine what an LP is worth?

CV: My basic criteria with pricing is three things and a couple of variables. Rarity is one, quality is the other, and demand is the other. And the issue of the record condition always comes into play but those are the three main things. Rarity probably being the most important. I think a lot of stores don't really understand pricing because they don't go to other stores. In one month I might go to sixty record stores, 200 thrift stores, eight flea markets, two record conventions. I know what's out there and what's not. There's records I see once a month and then there's records I see once every nine years. You just learn what's out there. And then there are just things that are regional, that are in that part of the country. Even major label stuff; there's some stuff in LA that's not in New York. It's those kind of things.

The pricing thing is also tricky for me because comparing some place like San Francisco to New York, there really is no comparison, because New York's like the center of the world—everybody meets there, everybody stops there. They can ask a lot more than I can. On the whole, in San Francisco, people just think they can find almost anything [for] under $10, and they just don't get that there are some things that you see and some things that you don't see. There is a contingent of new school diggers that just can't comprehend the value of a record. They might find an Al Hirt *Soul in the Horn* for a buck and then all of the sudden they are the fuckin' king of digging. They think it is all just that easy. Some people just can't differentiate a common record from something exotic and rare like the Saint Vincent Latinaires. The other thing is people sometimes don't acknowledge the luxury of a good selection. I personally would rather enter a store that had records priced $10 and up with a great selection, than sift through 25,000 crap records and come up empty-handed.

During San Francisco's big Internet boom, did you have a lot of dot-com millionaires suddenly coming into the store?

CV: Not at all. At the time, they'd come in and look for a Thievery Corporation record or something, but there was really only a few people with money that would come in and blow their money. They were more into CDs.

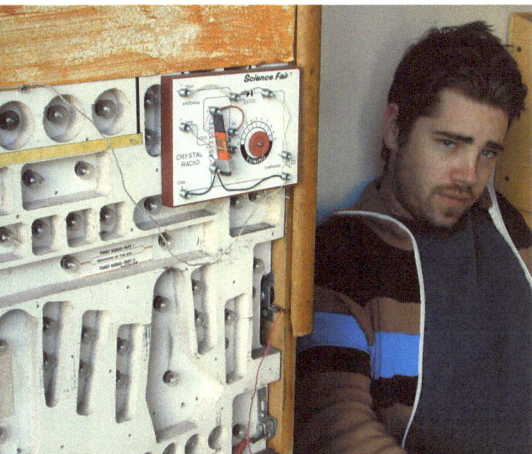

I know this is a topic that gets bandied about a lot, but as a storeowner, how do you deal with eBay and its impact on your store or just the collecting business in general?

CV: From a consumer standpoint, I have no problem with eBay. I think it can be a great thing. But from a business and a record store owner's standpoint, the cons far outweigh the pros. There are so many record stores that I go into nowadays that gauge their prices based on what somebody is paying on eBay. That's so wrong because there are only a few records that really stay at that point. There really is no rhyme or reason. When you start looking at records like stocks, it's just out of whack.

What has changed is that people are learning differently and I think the way a lot of the kids are learning is the wrong way. I get a lot of kids that are just getting into collecting, the same way that I did—through hip-hop or learning about samples—and they'll come in and it seems that eBay has brainwashed them into thinking that all the good things are going to pop up on eBay. They'll come in and they'll scoff at paying $75 for something off the wall, but then they'll turn around and they'll buy a record off of eBay because some jackass wrote, "Ill library beats with horn stabs"—and then they'll get this record and it fucking sucks. A lot of these kids are learning from pictures that are online.

When I was coming up, it was all about going over to somebody's house, trading records. I learned massively by trading and that's something I've always encouraged at the store, just bringing in trades. I think a lot of kids are basing what's good on what's going for a lot of money on eBay and I think that's really, really wrong. I just think they base too much on what they see and not what they hear. There's been records that I've seen on lists for years that I've always been curious about, but they're just not around and I've always wanted to hear them. It seems like a lot of kids will buy without ever hearing a record and it's unhealthy.

Other sources of annoyance?

CV: The most annoying trend I would say is picture book collectors and list collectors. There's this one guy who I hope will read this and completely stop coming into the store. He must be a buyer for some store and he comes with eighteen lists and a book, and he'll systematically go through the whole store, about once a month. About four hours sometimes, listening to stuff. He'll pull out tons of stuff but he references everything to his list and if it's not the exact same thing, he won't buy it. And he rarely buys anything. It doesn't matter what I have in the store, no matter how good the stock is, if it's not on his list, he doesn't buy it. I absolutely hate that shit. They're not buying for themselves—I have a problem with people who don't listen for themselves. I'm always thrown off when producers come in and ask me what's hot. I don't have any problems playing things for people I like, but if you're a producer and you're making music, how can I interpret [for] you what's good and what's hot?

Let's flip it around—what do you like best about your job?

CV: The hours are pretty good. [*laughs*] On my off days, I'm just out driving—I might be at a flea market or some place out of the city, looking for records—I like looking for records. It's a social job too; I just hang out and a lot of friends pop by. The store, business-wise, has always been so unpredictable; I've stopped thinking about it in terms of a retail space and it's more of just, kind of a hangout where I come, set up my records, and people come hang out, shoot the shit. That's what I like about it.

You ever worry that you're not going to be able to find good records to sell?

CV: As long as people get broke, there's always going to be records for sale. ◉

OLIVER WANG *is a freelance writer and DJ based in Oakland, CA.*

Cool Chris's "Top 20 That Make Me Tremble"
(in no particular order)

1. Klauss Weiss *Drums Around* (Select Sound)
2. Declaime "Flowers" 7-inch (Stones Throw)
3. Rolando Aguilo *Descarga Alegre* (Maype)
4. Tony Humphrey "Master Mix Medley" 12-inch (Westend)
5. Sharon Jones "Got a Thing on My Mind" 7-inch (Daptone)
6. TJ Swann "And You Know That" 12-inch (Express)
7. Boscoe *Self-titled* (Kingdom of Chad)
8. MC Jewel/DJ Screen "Reflection of Perfection" 12-inch (Hype)
9. J.C. Davis "A New Day" 7-inch (New Day)
10. Felix Del Rosario *Jazz Latino* (Borinquen)
11. Dub Diablo *The Shape Up* (DisJoint)
12. Burning Desire "Why She Had to Go" 7-inch (Charisma)
13. Pete Rock and CL Smooth "Back on the Block" 12-inch (BBE)
14. Gloria Jones "Tainted Love" 12-inch (AVI)
15. Caprells "Close Your Eyes" 7-inch (Bano)
16. Olli Ahvenlahti "Grandma's Rocking Chair (Kenny Dope Edit)" 12-inch (Jazzpu)
17. Blackalicious *Blazing Arrow* (MCA)
18. Whitefield Brothers "Chokin'" 10-inch (Soul Fire)
19. Kashmere Stage Band *Kash Register* (Kram)
20. M.C.P.S. "Mellow Mellow Ride On" 12-inch (Freedom Sounds)

MUSIC MOBILITY

by Oliver Wang
portables from Oliver Wang and Chris Veltri
photos by Jessica Miller

The beauty in portable phonographs is their mesh of form and function. Solid, innovative engineering remains the hallmark of the best portables such as the workhorse Columbia GP-3 or the sleek Audio Technica Mister Disc/Sound Burger. But once you get past the high-fidelity mechanics, portables also offered a feast for the eyes and not just ears. For the years of their popularity—roughly the 1950s through the early 1980s, the diversity of portable design reflects everything from the aesthetics of the lounge/jet era (Panasonic SG-338), to the miniaturized transistor craze (Takt Drifter), to space age mod (Philips "UFO" 22GF). Alas, CD technology all but made portable turntables an outdated artifact but leave it to the wax addicts to bring them back into vogue. Here are a few of Wax Poetics's favorite examples of these vinyl beat boxes.

Phono Book (maker unknown, circa 1960s)

This Japanese model is unusual insofar as it's designed to look like a book when stood closed and upright. Comes with a built-in AM tuner.

Drifter (Takt, circa 1960s)

One of the smallest portables capable of playing full-size LPs, the Drifter also comes with a built-in AM radio. It looks to be a dream for its tiny size, but its small motor has trouble playing LPs at consistent speed.

502 Attaché (Viscount, circa 1960s)

This small, squat portable boasts a slick mod-era design with its circular gauges that are visible through cut-outs in the cover.

SE-B "Lady Bug" (Columbia, circa 1970s)

More cute than functional (the cover doesn't store easily anywhere), the Lady Bug was later carried on—almost as an exact duplicate—by Radio Shack's Realistic line.

 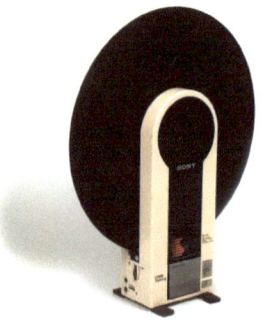

22GF "UFO" (Philips, circa 1970s)

This European model is one of the most striking, given its space-age design. Looks great, but its mass makes it clunky as far as portability goes. It's better left gracing your living room.

PS F5 (Sony, early 1980s)

This Sony model is designed to play upright, using an unusual liner tracking system (there is no tone arm). It's great in concept, but the linear tracking system is slow to jump between tracks.

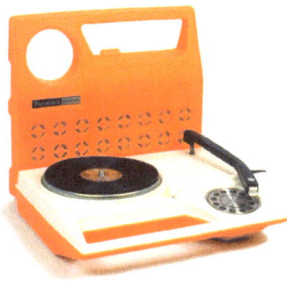

SG-338 (Panasonic, circa 1960s)

With its jet-era design and bright colors, it's simply one of the best-looking portables out there; also solidly engineered, complete with headphone jack.

Doral (circa 1960s)

Another player showing off mod-era influences, this larger portable comes with faux-wood paneling and chrome-plated tone arm.

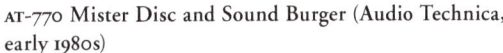

GP-3 (Columbia, 1990s)

One of the few portables in current production (and with pitch control), the sturdy GP-3 is produced out of Columbia's Japan division.

AT-770 Mister Disc and Sound Burger (Audio Technica, early 1980s)

Arguably one the best-designed portables, the AT-770 series (named according to where it was marketed worldwide) comes equipped with two stereo headphone jacks, twin RCA outputs, a 45 ring that doubles as a tone arm rest—even a headphone cord holder.

Sesame Street (Fisher-Price, 1983)

3814 (Fisher-Price, 1983)

These plastic-bodied turntables might look like cheap, children's toys, but for the money (usually less than $40), they are the most economical players on the used market.

waxpoetics 45

TEXAS FUNK SUNNY SIDE UP: BRUNCH WITH TIMOTHY MCNEALY

by Chad Burnett and Wilson Brooks

Geography is your friend. Use it to your advantage. If Detroit has the soul, San Fran has the psych, and London has the library, then Dallas has definitely got the funk. But just like anywhere else, it's no free lunch out here. Just because the history's here doesn't mean the Texas funk anthology is at your fingertips. However, with a little legwork and a lot of luck, it can be rather surprising what one can uncover. One day you're salivating over a super rare, super funky track off some bootleg comp, and the next day you're rapping about the tune with the original artist over a $2.99 breakfast buffet. Oh, the power of proximity!

Timothy McNealy lives an hour away. He is the legend who has given us the beautifully funky "Sagittarius Black" 45 with the equally brilliant "Funky Movement No. 2" on the flip. Perhaps the best-known release on his Shawn label, "Sagittarius" is only a tiny piece of this puzzle. We invite you to get the big picture by taking a stroll through the mind of one of the Lone Star State's funkiest. Come along with us, fellow diggers, it's time for the movement to commence.

BACKGROUND

Wilson: Prior to the launch of your label, what were you participating in musically?

McNealy: Well, I began playing professionally in 1956, at eleven years old. Several of us began quite young. My best friend was Michael Fugit—we lived in Sherman, Texas, and practiced in his parent's garage. We were using Sears amplifiers [Silver Tone] and a Fender Rhodes piano. The group was named Mike and the Six Sensations. We played for local club dances and were booked in other Texas clubs each weekend. Mike played bass. Charles Chamberlain played guitar and had a super feel for blues. Wallace Ray Polk and Ronnie Brewster played drums and were, what we called at that time, very funky. [Brothers] Charles and Fared Nibblet played tenor and alto saxes. I played piano and doubled out on slide trombone, something I had learned to play in public school. In or about 1963, after spending a short time in the Air Force, I returned to Sherman and re-joined the band. They had made a lot of progress and had a new band leader and trumpet player named James ["Bubba"] Fagin. Bubba had traveled on the road and had paid his dues, so to speak. His style was jazz and with his knowledge, we all were able to add to our musical abilities.

Chad: Were you involved with any other record labels before (or after) the creation of your own imprint?

I am one of the original members of the Mustangs, the backup band for Bobby Patterson [Jetstar Records]. In fact, I helped form the band. Two of my friends from Mike and the Six Sensations [Mike and Ronnie] were the first to be chosen and I was the bandleader until Robert ["Bobby"] Simpson joined the group. Bobby had a degree in music, so it was natural that he would take the lead spot in our group. I still played organ and helped record most of the tracks. I also contributed some vocals on a few of the songs. In fact, on the song "I'm Leroy, I'll Take Her," Bobby is talking to me. We were all in the same company with the Five Americans, and the owner's son had a group called John and Robin and the In-Crowd. At about the same time that Bobby Simpson started fronting the Mustangs, I was looking elsewhere to keep my music abilities polished. I remained a member of the band until around 1970, when John Abdnor, Sr. [of Abnak / Jetstar Records] dismantled us.

And one time [after the dismantling of the Mustangs] my band changed names to the Upsetters. We were well known in Dallas at that time. We had sessions under that name, although I don't remember much about what was recorded.

SHAWN EMERGES ON THE TEXAS SOUL SCENE

w: When was Shawn established? Have you always had sole ownership of the label and all of its publishing?

Shawn Records was founded in 1970. It was basically for my own personal use, primarily as an instrument to get my own music out. I have always owned it and my publishing [Sledge Publishing]. No one other than myself has ever owned any part of it at anytime.

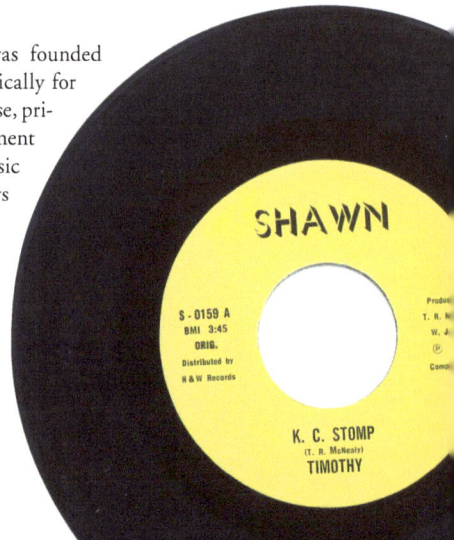

c: What is the significance behind the label's name?

Shawn is the middle name of my oldest son. His name is Timothy Shawn McNealy.

w: Did the distribution for Shawn records, through H&W One Stop, ever reach outside of Texas? Were there any other means for the distribution of your records?

At that time, H&W was the largest record dealer in the area. With a limited finance, I needed Walter Jackson, the owner of H&W, who was also a friend of mine, to help. He did, and that was the extent of my distribution. As far as out of state, I received news in 1972 that someone, even then, was black-marketing my records. I was a small company and had limited access to making an investigation.

[*WaxPoetics.com audio extra: McNealy gets news from Jabo Starks that "Sagittarius Black" is being bootlegged in NYC.*]

w: We know from previous questioning that "Funky Movement Pt. 2/Sagittarius Black" had a regular slot on the radio. Do you recall the station(s) from which your music was heard? What about radio stations in neighboring states?

It was played quite a bit here in Dallas. I don't recall the call letters, but I know that Houston, Austin, New York, California, Washington, and Jersey were just a few who had them on a regular play list.

c: Below is the Shawn discography, as we know it. Can you help us fill in any blanks, such as missing releases, b-sides, reference numbers, and/or release dates? And more specifically, we'd like to know if 0156 was your first release.

- Timothy McNealy "Will You Be There/Funky Movement" (Shawn 0156)
- Timothy McNealy "Funky Movement Pt. 2/Sagittarius Black" (Shawn 0157; 1972)
- Mr. B "Do It/What Would You Do" (Shawn 0158)
- Timothy "KC Stomp/Easy, Easy, Easy" (Shawn 0159)
- Timothy McNealy "What's Goin' On" (Shawn)
- Timothy McNealy "I'm Glad You're Mine" (Shawn)
- Rev. Timothy McNealy "Because of You/ Without You" (Shawn TM-203; 1981)
- Dr. Mack [Timothy McNealy] *Limited Edition* (Shawn 0173; August 2000)
- Dr. Mack [Timothy McNealy] *Don't Stop Praying* (Shawn 0177; November 2001)

S-0156 was the first record I released to the best of my knowledge. Through the years, you lose track of what, when, and where. Many of the numbers in between were never released and, until recently, I still had the three-inch masters of them all.

w: Out of the above titles, "KC Stomp" and "Funky Movement Pt. 1" seem to be the scarcest. We only know of one or two copies of each to be in existence. Were these 45s pressed on a significantly smaller scale than the other Shawn releases?

By the time I got my record company going, the cost of doing business was tough. Not a lot of money was there to press up a large amount of records. And even for a small company such as mine, things were hectic.

w: Do you remember how many copies were pressed for these two songs?

I only pressed 500 copies of each.

w: In regard to "Funky Movement Pt. 1" (Shawn 0156), we've heard it alleged that you don't remember cutting this specific song to record. How much truth does this statement hold?

I remember it, but it was not one of my favorites. If I heard it, I am sure I would remember much more about it.

[*We pause so that Mr. McNealy could recall this 45. Immediately after pressing play the memories start rushing back.*]

Oh yeah! I remember it now. That is definitely T-Bird Gordon on the horn. I haven't heard this in years! Back then we did a lot of track separation, so both the lead and backing vocals are mine. This was one of the main songs we would perform in the clubs at that time.

[*WaxPoetics.com audio extra: Listen to McNealy's reaction after hearing two long-lost tracks.*]

w: Tell us a little about the scene back then. The clubs had to be hoppin' at that time.

I guess one of the most exciting times was at a place called Soul City. It was out there on Greenville Ave. It was like a little Las Vegas club with the curtains and the big railing where people would sit around and order drinks and what have you. Then they had a floor space with tables that was right at the stage. And when the curtain opens you do your show. We were booked in there seventeen weeks straight in a row. And while we were there we were booked with acts like Dobie Gray, about the time he had his hit "I'm In with the In-Crowd." Also, Eddie Floyd came through and we did stuff behind him. I remember Jimmy Smith came in and performed, and we also got to play behind the Coasters. That was some of the most exciting times.

We were also doing a lot on the college scene. In Austin, we would go there to the university to perform for the sororities. We did that a few times. Then there was a time I was playing at Club Sands with Fred Alexander, who later played with Lakeside, and I remember we called our backing band Liquid Funk. After this I was playing at Rickshaw, which was a club over in North Dallas. It was heavy. When T-Bird Gordon was playing with me I called my band the Sweat Band. In fact, the Sweat Band was the band that played behind me when we recorded "Sagittarius Black" and "Funky Movement Part 2." So at one time in Dallas I had a pretty good name for myself. Folks knew I could play and if I had a band it was going to be together.

w: In addition to recording your solo material you recorded a 45 for Mr. B, "Do It/What Would You Do." Could you elaborate on this 45? We know Mr. B, aka Bernard Miller, was a FM radio DJ in Dallas, but how did you end up producing his record?

Well, Mr. B. was a young exciting radio jock that was hot on the FM station. One day I got a telephone call from him asking if I would help him record. Everyone I asked about him said that he was a good guy but that he could not sing. I was always a sucker for the underdog and open for a sob story, so I wrote and produced his material on my label. By doing this I learned I was strengthening my place in the radio programming. I also wrote some other songs at that time that I could never find again and I'll leave it at that.

SAGITTARIUS BLACK BAND
SHAWN RECORDING COMPANY

Backup Rhythm Section • Timothy McNealy
Sledge Publishing Co.
Photo By: T.McNealy © Copyright 1972

c: On your best-known 45, "Funky Movement Pt. 2" (Shawn 0157), I believe in the beginning of the song you shout "Lookout, Soultex!" This would obviously be directed towards the Dallas-based label of the same name? Can you tell us more about this rivalry of sorts with Roger Boykin's label?

Believe it or not, I said, "Look out, Joe Tex!" Joe was hot during those times and just mentioning his name was a ploy to be used.

w: Oops. We were hoping that would be our transition. Anyway, could you expand on your friendship with Mr. Boykin? We know you're good friends, but how long have you known each other? Did you know Roger at the time he was producing the Texas Soul Trio? Do you ever recall seeing Soultex artist Booker T. Averheart perform?

Roger and I met at clubs during the '60s where he was playing. It was mostly jazz, but very good jazz. We became good friends at that time and have remained close friends throughout the years. [In the] later years I asked him to play with me in the "What's Goin' On?" session. This was my interpretation of Marvin Gaye's hit tune and we both enjoyed it. Actually, it is still one of my favorite songs. Roger and I still keep in contact. In the early years, I had an opportunity to play several gigs with Booker T. Averheart. I didn't know him very well but he was a nice guy. I have not seen him in many years. I'd love to know what he's up to.

w: Your good relations have definitely lasted throughout the years. We've heard you on Mr. Boykin's 730 AM radio show that airs on Sunday afternoons here in Dallas. But besides Mr. Boykin's bands, who were some other notable local acts that were making noise around the same time you were?

[Rev.] Jimmy Filmore, Little Hamp, R. L. Griffin, Jolly George, Big Bo Thomas and the Arrows, Freddie Empire, Little Ernie, Big Jack Dixon, the Warm Excursions with Robert Whitfield, the Other Brothers, etc. During the '60s and early '70s, there were so many local artists battling for a spot and name recognition.

w: Digging a little deeper, did any local band(s) have any influence on your own sound?

There was a group by the name of Les Watson and the Panthers. I believe Willie Weeks was the bandleader's name. Those guys put on a real show. We began to hang out together and from this connection we both learned a great deal.

c: Did you ever travel out of Texas to perform? If so, where?

I traveled to many states, but the most exciting times were here in Texas. At that time I was more into my music than the girls, even though I still had more than my share. It was an amazing time! While with Bobby Patterson we were booked as the backup band in Houston for Bobby Sherman, who at that time had his own teen television show. This was definitely a crazy experience for us. So many women were there to see Bobby.

[WaxPoetics.com audio extra: McNealy backs teen idol Bobby Sherman; girls throw panties on stage during the show.]

w: Seems to me that at this time it was expected of you to know a lot of material. Did you have to learn the popular artist's songs in case a tour hit your town and needed a rhythm section?

Yes, we played a lot of shows for a lot of people. In spite of all that was going on, we looked at this as an opportunity rather than an inconvenience. We enjoyed performing for these artists. One of our hopes was to get recognized by a big-time producer and to get paid. We did have time to create our own tunes though. I'm telling you, it was a job back then. We would come to work at 8:00 AM, have a fifteen-minute break and a thirty-minute lunch, and the day would be over at 4:30 PM It was work!

REISSUES

w: Could you expand upon the business you've carried out with Soul Fire Records, the first company to legitimately reissue your material?

I have never met Phillip Lehman personally. I've only conducted business with him over the phone. A young collector from Alabama called me and made the connection between the two of us. We were able to agree on a deal and so came the reissue. He has also asked me to come to New York and play on some tracks with his band. It sounds like fun to me, but it has not happened yet. BBE also paid me some money and are currently paying royalties. The problem that I have no control over is if the people I am doing business [with] are being honest. I trust that they are and I leave it at that.

w: Speaking of Soul Fire, have you heard any of their new funk releases?

Phillip sends most of their stuff to me so I can get a real feel for the kind of stuff they do.

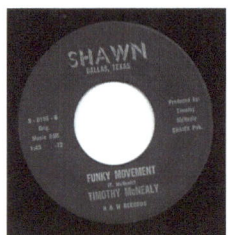

c: In these recordings, the main objective is to try to reproduce that late-'60s early-'70s sound. What is your view on this rough, analog approach in a time when polished, digital recording is the norm?

I think it's good in a sense but it locks us, the artists, in the past and fails to include our future. Musicians grow in their ability and knowledge. I think you know only part of the person if you accept only part of their work. It is almost impossible these days to make material that doesn't use some sort of digital instrument in the recording. The days are past for musicians to carry Hammond organs when there are so many lightweight keyboards to make the gigs.

w: Do you have any material, such as unreleased tracks, that have not been released yet? If so, are there any plans on doing so?

I have several tracks on two-inch and one-inch reels, but there are not many studios that have the equipment or capability to mix these old analog tapes. I do hope to remaster and release what I have left.

c: As far as the funk compilations go, have you been compensated by Soul Patrol for their use of your material?

During the Christmas holidays 2001, I was finally able to persuade Soul Patrol to fork up some money, but a bit short of what it should have been. I can appreciate the collectors in one way, but it is stealing when they do not do right with the artist. As an artist, it feels like someone has stolen a part of your life and is living it the way they want to. They don't care if you like it or not. Many artists are hungry with no place to live or can't pay their bills, while someone else has food, shelter, and is paying their bills with someone else's money.

LOSS OF MUSICAL POSSESSIONS

w: Word is that you are currently searching for some stolen property, including unreleased recordings, old photos, and other material belonging to you and the Shawn label. Could you tell us a little bit about the perpetrator(s) and how they were able to get hold of your possessions?

A young man by the name of Erik Jung came to my home in search of material that had not yet been released. The local television station made a big story about his coming here, at my request. They interviewed him at my home. It was an honor, so I thought, to have this gentleman visit me at my house. I treated him to a great lunch, in which my friend Roger Boykin joined us. I put a lot of trust in him. Besides, I was loaning him almost all my old stuff, or at least what I had left at the time. He assured me that his intentions were for the good. I felt a need to protect my material, since we would be doing business from such a far distance. We decided it would be best to come up with some sort of contract. This was my way of protecting my property. I was to get a contract in the mail the following week. This never took place. He was to make copies of the photos that I had let him borrow and then return the originals. This also never happened.

While he was at my home he told me only part of his story and he assured me that the materials were to be on loan only. I had no reason not to trust this man. Well, the days grew longer with the least bit of contact coming from Erik. When I realized that he was taking too long to do what he promised I simply asked [for] my materials to be sent back at once. He refused to do so and stopped calling and sending emails altogether. I'm optimistic that I will eventually get my belongings back. If he'd just return my material, that would be the end of it. Although with the time that has passed, it seems I might have to go after him with a lawsuit. It sure is a shame.

SHAWN 2002

w: Since I've been talking to you, I've gathered that you have continued to produce new recordings on the Shawn label. Could you talk about the musicians/projects that are currently on your label and what will be released in the near future?

Currently all the music I am doing are tracks of myself. Having track separation allows me to do all the instruments. Recently, though, I have begun working with some local musicians and it is my hope that some good things will develop from our work. I have several projects, which are all contemporary gospel: The Angelic Voices, James Bolin, and Susie Vairs Andrews. They don't have a lot of stage experience but [have] real potential. They perform at local functions like parties, funerals, and weddings.

w: Any final statements, thoughts, announcements, or outright plugs before we wrap this up?

I look forward to appearing in the UK and meeting some of the hundreds of people who have sent me emails about my material. I also want to thank you for thinking enough of me and for extending a hand of friendship. Thank you and God bless. ◐

CHAD BURNETT *digs, drinks, samples, and sleeps when he's not working for the Man. Occasionally he pretends he has a bachelor's degree in journalism and submits material to magazines.* WIL BROOKS *is that dude who sits off to the side and observes everything—a very complex man: devoted to God, so records come second…third, fourth, and fifth. As a team, they record music as Rehash; their style can be seen at RehashMedia.com, and their sounds bought at TurntableLab.com.*

photos by the authors

TAPE CHECK… WITH KON AND AMIR

by Reeve Hohlt
photos by Michael Spears

Spurred by a desire to let the world know that there was no one king of digging, and to share with the masses the assorted sampled gems in their crates, Kon and Amir released their seminal *On Track* tape in early 1997. Since then, they've released three more lauded volumes, with number five on the way. The success of the tapes has blessed them with the opportunity to build with many of the producers whose own discoveries inspired them, forced Amir to sign an autograph (with the requisite corny inscription "keep digging"), and even brought some dusty-fingered hate their way.

Why did you start making the tapes?

Kon: Basically, we just got together and decided that, you know, we knew a lot of the original sources for the music that was coming out that we were kind of fans of at the time, and basically it'd be nice [for people] to listen to.

Amir: Yeah, and I mean the way I look at it is, the reason we kind of did it is, before we did our tape there was that cat DJ Muro from Japan who was calling himself the king of digging, and when we used to listen to his tapes—they were cool, they had some good stuff on 'em, but it was like, "B, you're not the king of digging."

K: Yeah, and [we weren't] trying to be kings either; we [were] just doing it 'cause we love it.

One of the only tapes like *On Track* that I knew of before yours was Shame's *Traveling Through Sample Land*. Besides Shame and Muro, who else was making tapes before you two?

A: I can't think of anybody at all.

Was Shame's tape an influence in putting the first tape out?

K: I wouldn't say an influence as far as the tape being put out, but Shame's tape was definitely influential as far as maybe *making* a tape. Not necessarily putting it out and going about trying to sell it to people, but just actually putting it to tape to listen to and, you know, just vibe with—sure. When Shame first did that tape, though, at the time, I was already doing the same thing he was doing. The first time I met him was like in '91 at Avenue C [in Boston], and he came up to me while I was playing ["Upon This Rock" by] Joe Farrell—at the time it was [sampled by] Black Sheep for "Flavor of the Month"—and he was like, "Yo, you're doing this too." So, it wasn't really like, *let's bite Shame*.…To tell you the truth, I wasn't even really thinking about other people's shit.

Since the tapes focus so heavily on samples, what resources do you two utilize to identify the records that artists have used?

A: Well, I know for me at least, every time we get ready to do a tape I just go through all the records in my collection first, and I see what I have that somebody used already—before I go to any record store. And, you know, I think one of the advantages that we have since we first put out our tape is that people are just—people that are fans of ours, of our tapes—they just come up to us and be like, "Yo, did you know so and so used this?" and I'm like, "Word?" They just volunteer information to us.

K: Yeah, word of mouth.

A: So it's like, for those who did that, thank you very much.

K: No doubt.

A: People have even volunteered their records to us, like, "Yo, if you can't find it I'll give you the record so you can use it on the tape." And, by the way, thank you for that too.

Are there any samples either of you want to know but don't?

K: Yeah, I want to know what the original to "Shook Ones" is.

A: Yeah, everybody wants to know that.

K: I'd like to know.

A: Supposedly, Prodigy found that record, and they made that record in their bedroom or some shit like that. And I heard that Havoc is not the type of person that would tell someone what that is. So, you know, no one really knows what that record is.

K: What about Beatnuts "No Escaping This"?

A: Yeah, that too.

K: What is that? You know that's a cheesy record. Whatever it is, it's some corny record—it definitely doesn't sound like no funk.

Speaking of corny records, clearly in the digging world, rarity and demand begets value, but what highly valued records do you think are really overrated?

A: Well, I would say one record, to come off the top of the head—I don't necessarily think it's a garbage record but it's not a record that I would [want]—and I used to own the record, actually—is the Third Guitar 45. You know, "Baby Don't Cry." When you see that online go for six to seven hundred dollars, you know what I'm saying, as a 45, I think that shit is ridiculous. You know people are going crazy over it because, number one, it was on *Brainfreeze*, and number two, Large Professor used it for Main Source. To me, it's not that rare of a 45 for people to get crazy over, and the music in the song is [just] *okay*.

Any others come to mind?

K: Shit, half them records on the wall when you go to New York [record shops].

Despite some of the current nonsense involved with digging—like crazy prices—and despite the fact you've been doing this for a while, do breaks still blow your minds?

A: Yeah.

K: The thing that blows my mind is when I think someone really got busy with a sample and chopped shit up, and come to find out they just looped it.

Any good recent examples?

K: Yeah, I would definitely say that Jadakiss joint ["We Gonna Make It," produced by Alchemist]; I thought he chopped that up.

Of course that's on the new tape, right?

K: Yeah. No doubt. ◯

Reeve Hohlt (aka DJ Bill Bixbee) is originally from Brooklyn. When not investigating crooked cops for his nine-to-five, he contributes to URB, *and DJs around New York.*

the elite 20
a selection of some of the most wanted hip-hop records in the world
by chris aylen

Having spent many of my years listening to hip-hop, my devotion to the music has led to an equal obsession of maintaining a collection of key and rare pieces of wax. Growing up, saving pocket money and newspaper delivery wages to buy the latest albums and singles formed a large part of my childhood. An album would last me months of continual play before I bought something new. It wasn't until I started working full time that I began to try and track down the wax that I'd missed. Filling the gaps in my racks became an important pastime, and trawling record fairs filled up many weekend mornings.

Enter the Internet. Until 1997, I hadn't even investigated the possibilities out there on the web. (In '99, I picked up on the whole eBay phenomenon: At last there was a resource where every imaginable record could turn up for sale.) A little searching led me to other collectors' websites. Every one of them had a want list comprised of various records. Some I'd heard of, some I hadn't, and some I already had myself. But there is a fairly consistent stock of titles that have graced almost every collector's list—whether the list exists mentally, digitally, or is simply scrawled onto notepaper—and it is these pieces that I'm focusing on here. All of these records exist and all of them do turn up from time to time on dealers' lists, the Internet, or in your local junk store. Let's get this started right.

All of the following records are either from my own collection or borrowed from the resources of Rare Dave, DJ Bombjack, and the Sound Library, and are featured in no particular order.

Main Source "Think/Atom" 12-inch (Actual Records) 1989

The debut Main Source record featured the young Large Professor alongside "those two DJs," Sir Scratch and K-Cut (who was known as Kay Cut at the time). Rumored to be the first release off the forthcoming album, *The Main Source Breaks the Atom*, the group switched from the indy label Actual to Wild Pitch after the second single ("Watch Roger Do His Thing/The Large Professor") and released the debut album *Breaking Atoms* to much acclaim.

This single has been bootlegged in a variety of guises, but the original pressing has a darker red label than the boots and has the Specialty Record Corporation (SRC) logo stamped into the runout. An original pressing will usually sell around the $200 mark depending on condition.

The Beatnuts "Fried Chicken/Hellraiser (remix)" 12-inch test pressing (Relativity) 1994

Although often mentioned in lists as a promo, this is actually a test pressing that was sent to a-list DJs in 1994. "Fried Chicken" is the same as the LP version (albeit with radio and instrumental versions as well—and minus that annoying skip that was on the original US LP vinyl pressing), but the remix of "Hellraiser" is very nice. The version of "Hellraiser" on *The Beatnuts* album cuts off at the end with a different beat—and it's that beat that graces the whole of this promo remix.

This record was bootlegged with a yellow label soon after, but this original pressing remains a pinnacle piece in most collectors' lists.

Big Daddy Kane "Ain't No Half Steppin'" 12-inch promo (Cold Chillin') 1988

Another record that everyone seems to have in their lists is this promo-only single with the vocal remix of "Ain't No Half Steppin'." Very similar to the original mix from the *Long Live the Kane* album, the only difference is how the "UFO" sample is extended and treated slightly differently—and despite the label reading 6:19, this is still just over five minutes in length.

Another particularly nice feature of this record is the instrumental on the flipside. One of the rarest records—and subsequently one of the most-wanted.

Pete Rock and CL Smooth "The Creator/Mecca and the Soul Brother" 12-inch promo (Elektra) 1992

This promotional single features the remixes of "The Creator" (the Surfboard Mix with the hard drums and the standard Slide to the Side Mix from the *Mecca and the Soul Brother* album), but the main reason to dig this out is the Wig Out Mix of "Mecca and the Soul Brother." A full minute and a half longer than the standard version, this takes the original track somewhere completely different.

A rare piece that always seems to sell for a lot of money.

De La Soul *Clear Lake Auditorium* EP promo (Tommy Boy) 1994

A great EP pressed in a batch of 500 and given out by Tommy Boy after the release of the *Buhloone Mindstate* album, this features four previously released tracks and the unavailable "Sh. Fe. MC's" joint with A Tribe Called Quest. On the flipside, you also get "Stix & Stonz" with Grandmaster Caz, Whipper Whip, Tito from the Fearless Four, LA Sunshine, and Superstar, making a bizarre-but-excellent exclusive track.

This has been bootlegged on black vinyl and more recently on clear vinyl to mimic the original pressing, but the original comes in a clear plastic sleeve and has a green tinge to the vinyl.

Lord Finesse & DJ Mike Smooth "Baby, You Nasty" 12-inch (Wild Pitch) 1989

One of the rarest commercially released singles, this was the great Finesse's first 12-inch from his debut album. The version of "Baby, You Nasty" on here is different than the album version and DJ Premier's production here proved him a force to be reckoned with. The flipside is "Track the Movement," also produced by Primo.

Surprisingly elusive for a commercially available single.

Diamond D "Sally Got a One Track Mind" 12-inch promo (Chemistry) 1993

Although technically this is by Diamond and the Psychotic Neurotics, we still all know and love him as Diamond D. This promotional version of the "Sally" single features an exclusive DJ Mark the 45 King remix of "Best Kept Secret," which is officially unavailable anywhere else.

Strangely enough, I usually see the test pressing more often than this sticker-covered promo.

Big Willie Smith *Da Beat Terrorists* EP (Funky Ass Records) 1995

Five hundred copies of this four-track EP were pressed exclusively for the non-US market by Kool Keith (under the pseudonym of Big Willie Smith) on his own label. Since then, it has become a folklore-ish piece, mainly due to the fact that Keith has denied its existence in previous interviews. Kutmaster Kurt lends his production skills here, and Keith's fans will recognize the track "Keep It Real, Represent" from his excellent *Sex Style* album that followed soon after.

This EP has since been bootlegged with black and white labels.

Nas "Life's a Bitch" 12-inch promo (Columbia) 1994

One of the stranger promotional-only singles, as it looks shop-ready with a full-color picture cover and the commercial Columbia red record labels on the vinyl. The bonus on here is the Arsenal Mix of "Life's a Bitch," which is only available on this single.

Very rare in the original form, this always sells for good money. Bootlegged recently, but fairly easy to spot the differences (muddy picture scan on the cover and wrong font on the labels)—and the promotional original never came shrink-wrapped, so if you see something along those lines you'll know it's the "reissue."

Jeru the Damaja "Da Bichez" 12-inch promo (Payday) 1994

One of the more relaxing tracks from the excellent *The Sun Rises in the East* album, this was put out as a single on a promotional basis only. Two different pressings exist from the same time, with one having the word "instrumental" spelled incorrectly on the label.

K-Solo "Your Mom's in My Business" 12-inch promo (Atlantic) 1990

The remix of one of the more popular K-Solo tracks is only available on this promotional single. The first pressing has a simple black and white label, while the second is the finished promo with the standard Atlantic green, orange, and cream bands on the label.

Very rare and a popular want among diggers, despite the remix not being that different to the original mix.

Common "The Bitch in Yoo" 12-inch promo (Relativity) 1996

The main track from a Relativity compilation album, this promotional-only 12-inch has Common (Sense) verbally destroying Ice Cube over an amazing Pete Rock beat. Although Common and Cube have long-since squashed the beef, this track remains one of the hardest hitting dis tracks of the past decade of hip-hop music.

Exists as two different official pressings, but has also been bootlegged.

Showbiz & A.G. *Party Groove/Soul Clap* EP (London/Payday) 1992

One of the best debut records ever, this EP introduced the DITC crew to many heads worldwide and secured its place in the annals of hip-hop history. The first version was released independently by Showbiz himself and has a slightly different track listing.

Eight tracks deep, this has since been reissued in a variety of forms—the original has a full picture cover and a sticker on the front; usually sells for $100.

Wu-Tang Clan "Protect Ya Neck" 12-inch (Wu-Tang Records) 1992

Another classic debut single: how many of you can remember the first time you heard this? An amazing record that has held its weight over the past decade—and remains one of the best tracks ever recorded by the Staten Island crew.

The first pressing of this record has no barcode on the label and sells for around $100. Then there's a second pressing (with the barcode) on this same label. And then you'll find the Loud pressings with the black and white picture cover as well.

Marley Marl "Marley Marl Scratch" 12-inch (NIA) 1985

In the typical "homage to the DJ" styles of the mid-'80s, MC Shan lets everyone know why Marley's the king over one of the most basic-but-effective drum patterns ever. After being featured on *Ego Trip*'s excellent *The Big Playback* compilation, we witnessed this shoot up in value to around the $80 mark. Classic hip-hop and a key piece in anyone's collection.

waxpoetics 55

Eminem *Slim Shady EP* (Web Entertainment) 1998

Not technically the full EP by any means, but this single featured "Just Don't Give a Fuck," "Low Down, Dirty," and the original DJ Head Mix of "Just the Two of Us" (which is the main reason for everyone wanting this). Since Em's popularity has blown up, all his earlier material has become very collectable.

Very rare even at the time of release, this 12-inch has been subsequently bootlegged, and always sells for a lot of money regardless of how legit the pressing is.

Lifers Group/DJ Shadow "Real Deal/Lesson 4" 12-inch promo (Hollywood BASIC) 1991

The Lifers Group released all their music from jail and never seemed to succeed commercially, but Hollywood BASIC sowed the seeds for the DJ Shadow phenomenon by having him produce this promo-only remix for one of the Lifers tracks. On the flipside was Shadow's own nod of respect to Double Dee and Steinski in the form of "Lesson 4," which has since become a modern-day classic example of the cut-and-paste technique.

Heavily bootlegged (and very well executed), the original with its "HIP HOP on the HIP HOP tip with a HIP HOP appeal to it" etching in the run-out grooves is worth around $200+. The OG pressing also has a Lifers Group sticker on the white promo sleeve.

Pete Rock and CL Smooth "Searching/We Specialize" 12-inch (East West Japan/Elektra) 1996

This Japan-only release features the original version of the already promo-only "Searching" single—but then adds an exclusive remix and another unreleased track on the b-side in the form of "We Specialize." A great single that all Pete Rock and CL fans should own.

Unity Committee and Rebels of Rhythm "Unified Rebelution" 12-inch (No Label) 1994

Recorded by Unity Committee and Rebels of Rhythm (better known to all as Jurassic 5 today), this single was pressed up on a strictly limited basis (less than 500) and then given another small repress for the Mr. Bongo shop in London. There's this original pressing with the yellow label, the second pressing with a blue label, and then a pressing on Blunt Records with a picture cover and a different track listing.

Gang Starr "Jazz Thing" 12-inch promo (Columbia) 1990

Another heavily bootlegged record, this Gang Starr track laid down the blueprint for many jazz/hip-hop records released afterwards, although few people executed it so well. Taken from the *Mo' Better Blues* film, Branford Marsalis and DJ Premier provide the perfect backdrop for Guru to speak about the history of jazz music.

Released with a picture cover in the UK, there are two official US promo versions with slightly different track listings—and a whole host of bootleg copies floating around.

And there you have a small list of some of the most wanted joints around. Avoid the pitfalls of the bootleg and spend a little time digging around and you'll more than likely come up trumps on some of these pieces. Good places to start are by asking other collectors and by checking out stores such as the Sound Library and your local second-hand spot. If you're confident of the seller, the Internet can be a great place to find some of the rarer pieces, but buying online is always a poor substitute for digging out the vinyl after hours of going through crates and boxes in a junk shop.

Never forget the cardinal rule: a record is never great because of its rarity value. Good music is good music, simple and plain. ◍

CHRIS AYLEN *contributes to* SpineMagazine.com, *does design and illustration for UnorthodoxStyles.com, and buys his sneakers at CrookedTongues.com. When he's not on eBay buying records under various pseudonyms, you can find him hanging out with his puffer fish, Uncle Remus.*

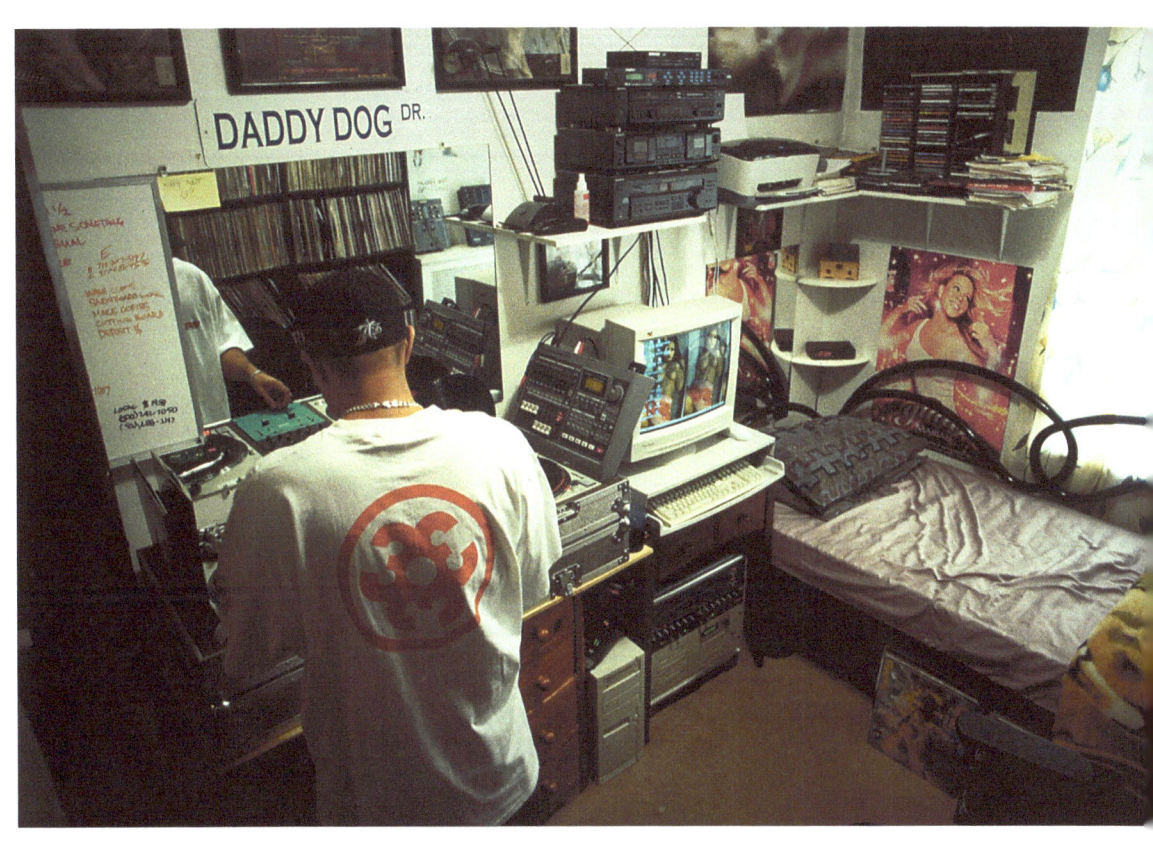

IN THE BEDROOM
a photo essay by John Carluccio

DJ PRECISION
Corona–Queens, NY

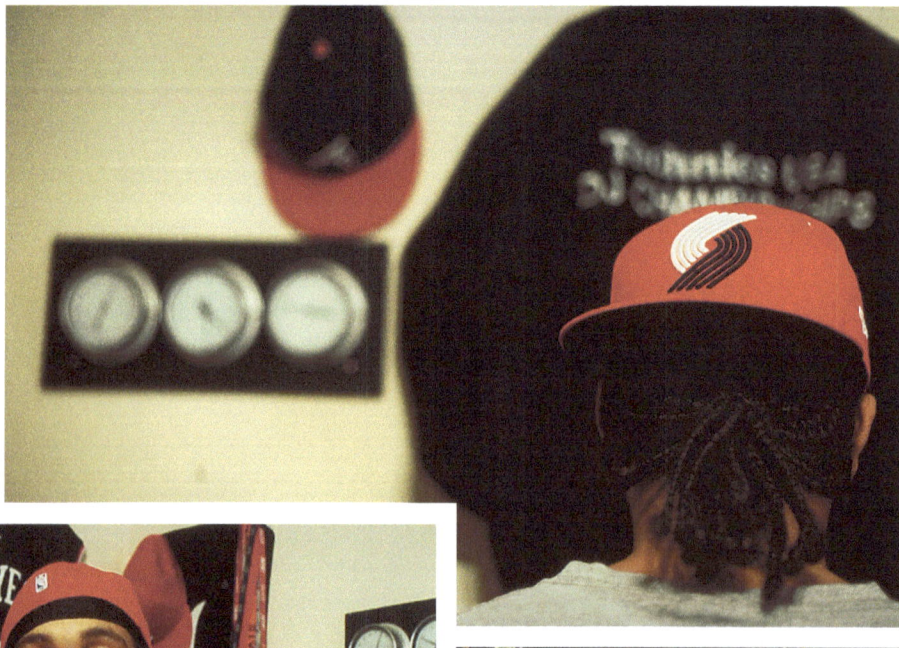

New York

JORDAN
CITY

MUTOMBO
55

GLOBAL B-BOY CONNECTION
PRESENTS
BATTLE OF THE ILLEST

$ 2,000
Technics

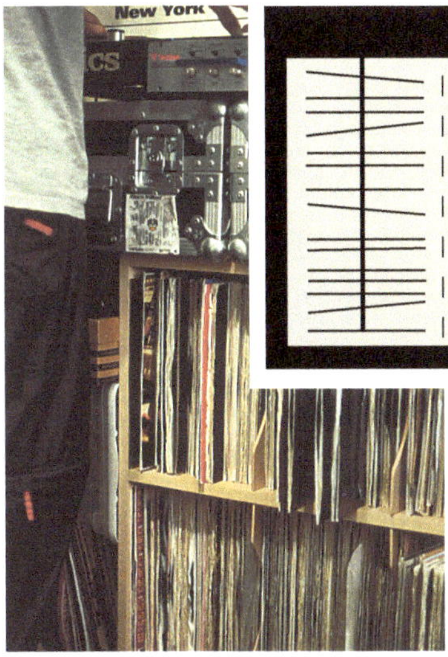

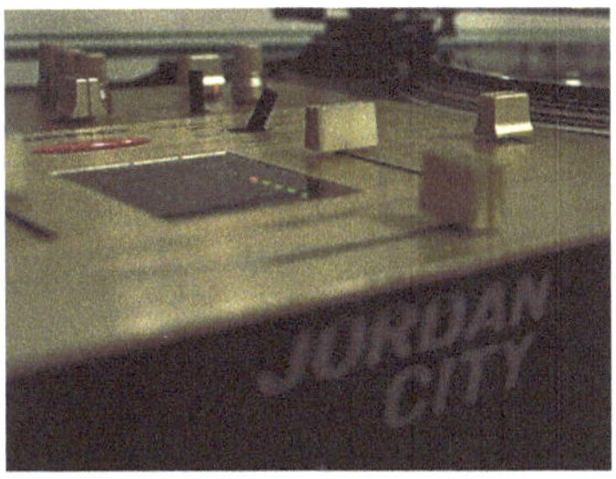

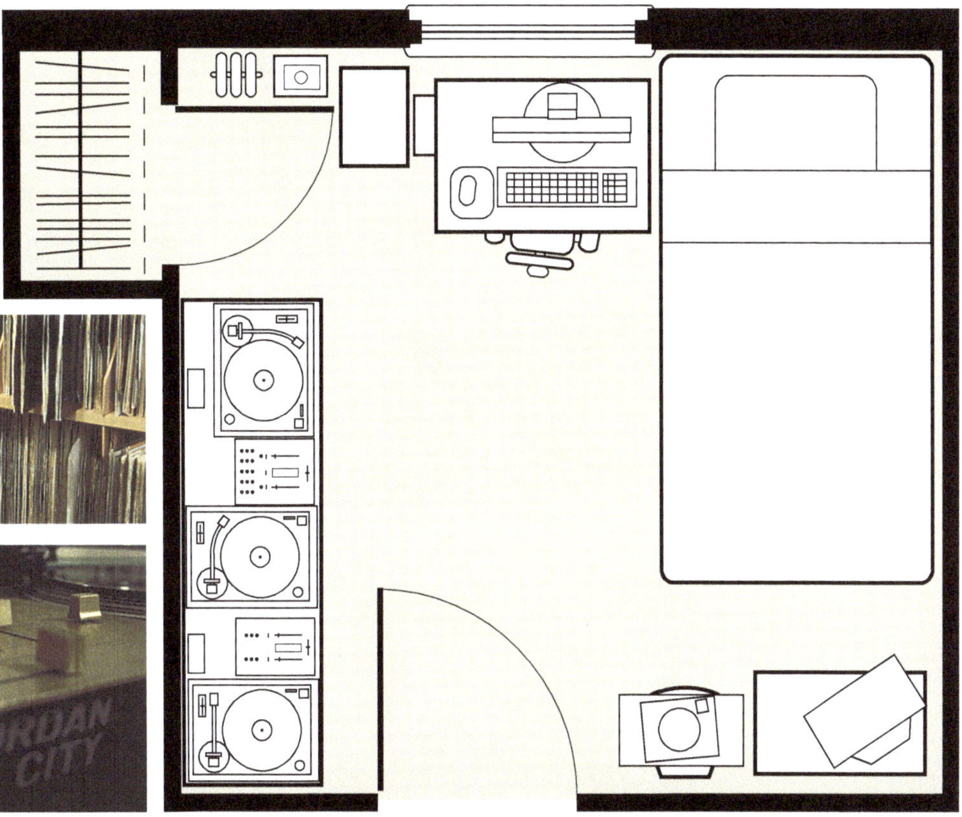

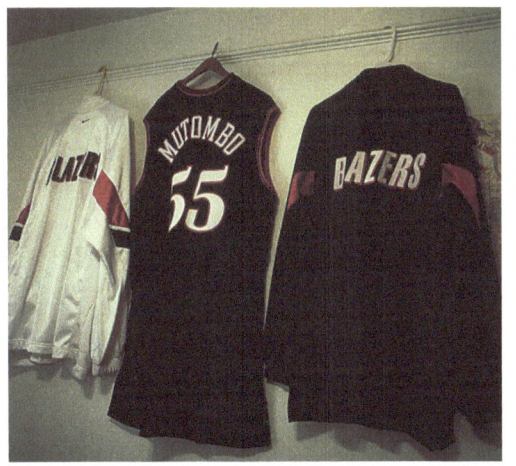

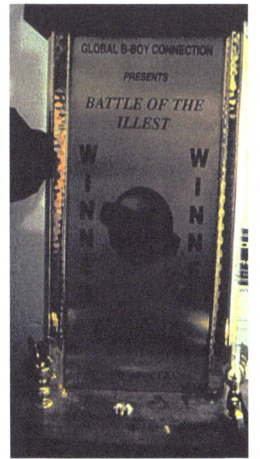

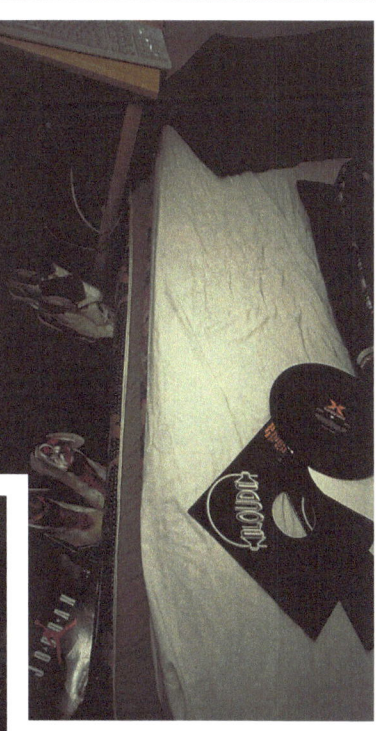

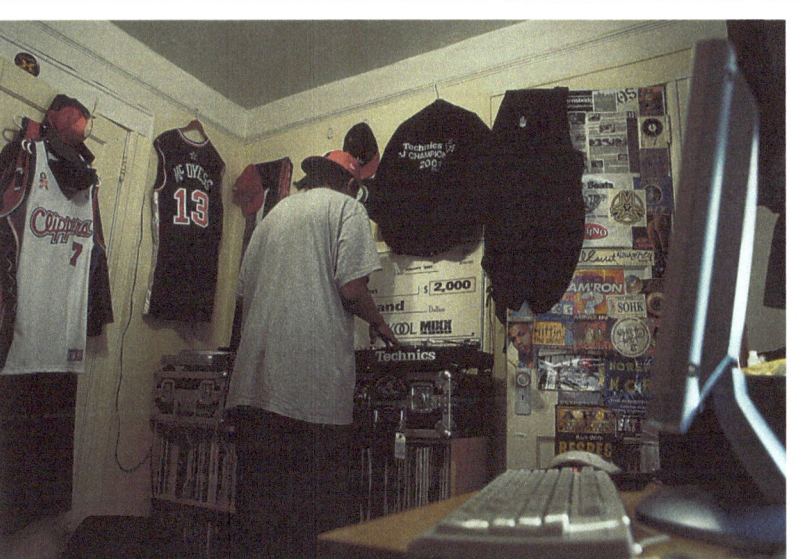

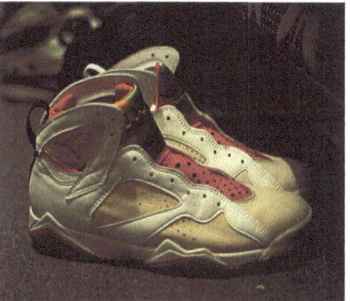

DJ IXL
Bushwick–Brooklyn, NY

BEFORE

too many people sitting on his bed

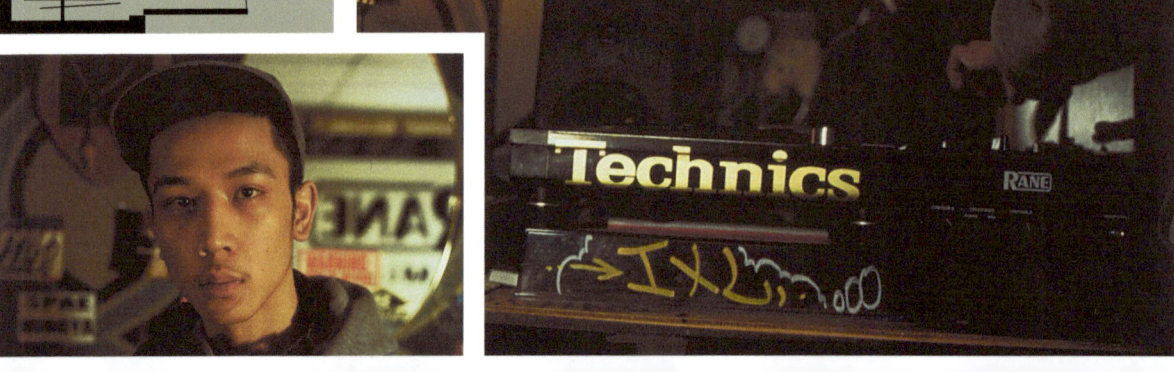

NOW
moved bed out.
sleeps over girlfriend's place.

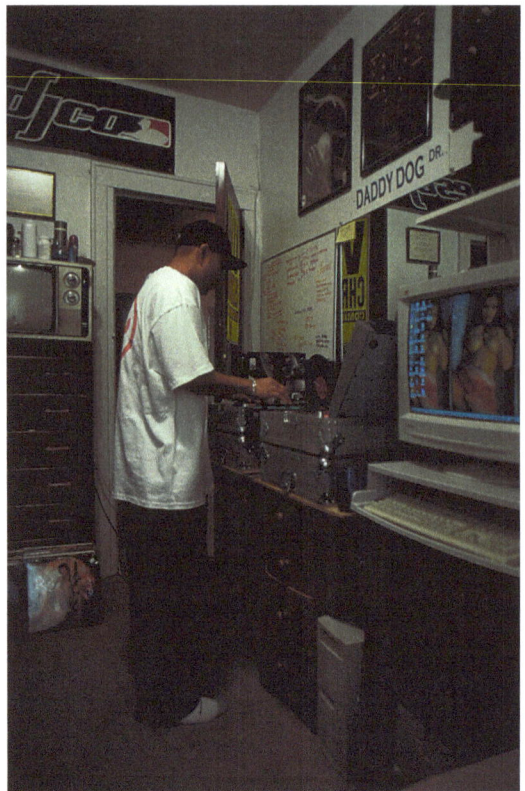

DJ DADDY DOG
Jackson Heights–Queens, NY

The Human Element: Malcolm Catto

by Zaid

photos by Monika Magiera

When you're looking for Malcolm Catto, and you've arrived in the deepest reaches of North London one night, found the right pitch-black alleyway and gone down it as instructed, only to end up in what appears to be an uninhabited area of garages, it's best to play it by ear. Follow the only sound emanating from the otherwise dead-end situation—the magnetic and, though faint, unmistakable hum of a drum kit being pounded relentlessly—up a staircase, and wait. Because, until he stops playing, he can't hear you knocking.

Though the first room you see upon entering his flat is scarcely brighter than the darkness you traverse to reach his front door, it's a sight to behold. Apart from the drums, the large space is consumed by all manner of dusty musical apparatus and oddments—amps, speakers, guitars, keyboards, recording devices, and a wealth of unidentifiable, bulky machinery. This is the lab of Malcolm Catto: funk collector of considerable note, creator of the Mo' Wax album *Popcorn Bubblefish*, and drummer with the Soul Destroyers—THE HEAVIEST AND WILDEST FUNK BAND IN THE WORLD TODAY, according to the gig poster on his wall. We thought we'd go 'round and talk about his work and some of the stuff he's reissuing on his label, Funk 45. Malcolm, however, had other ideas.

How did you come to connect with Mo' Wax?

It started off that I'd done a 10-inch for ["Jazzman"] Gerald's label, Stark Reality. I think it was gonna be the first thing on the label, but it was pretty bad when I look back on it. [*laughs*] Some of it was alright, but he played it around to a few people and they were saying it wasn't the right move, especially not for the first release, so they didn't bother putting it out. This is going back a few years now; some of the stuff is on the Mo' Wax LP but in a different guise. It was all done on four-track, so it sounded fucking rough—I'd just got it and I was too keen on just putting down music rather than working out how to use it. Anyway, there was only about four of these pressed up. Maybe ten at the most. Gerald sent a few off to Badly Drawn Boy and people like that for their opinions, and they said, "No, don't bother with it," which was the general consensus. There was one [at] his market stall, and James [Lavelle] came 'round, said, "Oh, what's new?" like he does, and they played him that. I phoned him up and said, "Are you interested in putting some of that out?" and he said, "Yeah, okay." Lavelle just thought he'd take a chance on it. Never really saw it as a commercial venture. And I don't blame him! It was never that sort of thing.

So it was all done on 4-track?

Mainly, yeah. I've only really just picked this up [*motioning to the equipment strewn around*] recently. I'm still working out how to wire it all up. There's so many problems involved with old equipment, like earth hums, and I don't have a fucking clue about that sort of thing.

Did they give you the freedom to do whatever you liked?

They had a few suggestions, obviously, 'cause some of it was getting pretty odd. And from a commercial point of view for a record company, that can be the kiss of death. So he did say on a few things—"Calm that down a bit"—but in the end I think he got a bit pissed off with dealing with me and just said, "Oh, fuck it, do what you want." [*laughs*] There were a few things that he vetoed and said, "I'm not putting that out." But it's as good as I could do with the equipment, and playing it all on my own. Ideally, I'd get a band who are better musicians than me to play it all. I mean, I can just about justify myself as a drummer, not as a bass player, guitarist, or keyboard player, you know? There was a sound I had in my head and no one was doing it, so I thought I'd just fill that gap if I could. But there's a lot of stuff that didn't get released—jazzier soundtrack stuff that I quite liked, but it was too jazzy for Mo' Wax. They didn't wanna take it down that path at all. I spent a lot of money on horn sections, jazzing it out, you know? On your own it's a bit hard, though, 'cause I haven't got a sampler. Without that, you've got to get a tight take of everything you're playing. It's so much easier just looping yourself, but then again it loses something by that as well. Ideally, you just wanna have a band that can do it all live.

> THERE WAS A SOUND I HAD IN MY HEAD AND NO ONE...

  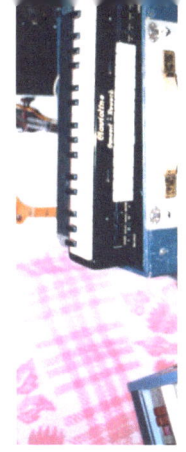   

You couldn't find the musicians?

Pretty much. I was working with other guys but it just took so long, and no one really heard it the same way as me. So in the end, I just thought, fuck it, I'll do it myself and be closer to what I'm after. But yeah, it is pretty ragged in places. But I [wasn't] able to take it all and edit it on the computer and stuff like that until a later date, and I was out of money, so I could only do a few tracks, and I was fucked then, really. There's a couple that are edited where I took the best bits, looped them up and added stuff on top. But mostly it's just live stretches, taking out things that went horribly wrong.

I'm not really after something click-tight. I want it to be tight, but I'd rather it had a human feel. Because everything *is* click-tight—you just turn on the telly and there's breaks on adverts, and there's something not very human about it. You know, you listen to some of the old sevens, and the playing is fucking brilliant—the level of musicianship. And a lot of them were about fifteen when they made these records. Some of it, consequently, is a little bit, you could say, sloppy, but the human element, I think, is more important than having it click-tight so a DJ can mix into it. It just comes from the soul a bit more rather than a computer. And it kills hip-hop, a little bit, when you see it on a computer, just looping over. But they've got the rapping as the soul element, injecting their personalities with the rapping, I suppose. Y'know, I love hip-hop. I listen to it as a band—imagining a band where you've got Bernard Purdie, Paul Chambers, Lou Reed…all these guys from totally different backgrounds, just all together and playing. And they're not worried if something doesn't quite go, or if it's not exactly in concert pitch. It doesn't matter, it creates an intriguing effect by not being like that sometimes.

How did you find the transition from making music designed for 45s to an album format? Stylistically, *Popcorn Bubblefish* doesn't sound like the Soul Destroyers.

Well, I like the idea of a seven because it's good discipline. You know, to have three minutes rather than twenty minutes. You listen to a seven, and they've got so much in it, because for a lot of these guys it was their only chance to be heard so they put everything they had into three minutes.

In this day and age, with people's attention span being about thirty seconds, they want something instantaneous. Not that I'd want to give it to them, but I do like the mentality of sevens, yeah. Hitting people with something that's concise. That's the thing with a lot of hip-hop—there's no changes in it, or if there are they come after a long time, whereas with a seven you've got half a minute then there's a change. It just keeps you interested, and, like I said, it's exciting because it's human.

The way I did [*Popcorn Bubblefish*] was that I was trying to do different bands. Just one production style on an LP bores me a bit, to be honest, unless it's *The White Album* or something. But generally, everything's so polished now so I thought I'd go for loads of different character styles. Again, it is a bit of a sevens mentality. I'd love to have strong enough songs just to do one really good production [style], but I'm not really into songs for songs' sake. The [formula of] verse, chorus, verse, middle eight, it's been done to death; I'd love to try and break out of that if I can. But the thing that's gonna make you different from someone else is your influences. One of my influences is printing—that's what I do by trade, I'm a qualified printer. Listening to all the noises in the factory, of all the different printing machines on their own different timings, you know? It's hypnotic.

What else do you love about the funk sevens?

I love the way they put it together rhythmically. That's the trouble with a lot of the funk bands today—they don't really make full use of the different rhythms that you can put over something, 'cause it ain't just coming from the drums. Say you've got a 4/4 beat, there's so many counter-rhythms you can put over that. That's the problem sometimes with the Soul Destroyers as well—I was listening to a tape of a gig we'd done, and it was *so* straight. What me and the bass player was putting down was quite tight, and what you could put over that is endless. We're getting better, but I think a few of us are still stuck in that, *it's got to be funk* [mentality], and

> …WAS DOING IT, SO I THOUGHT I'D JUST FILL THAT GAP.

that's when it fucks up because you're *never* gonna come up with something as good as some of that stuff. Never. It was a certain time and mindset that can't be repeated. One of the problems with music over here is that there's nothing much to rebel against. We've got it so easy. Back then, they had everything to rebel against. They still have; that's what surprises me about hip-hop—they're eating each other in the ghettos and not focusing their anger on what the real problem is: the government. They're just doing exactly what the government would want them to do, which is fight amongst themselves and not face the real problems that are higher up.

The trouble with a lot of modern music is that people think, *Oh, you've got to follow this formula to make money.* That's not the way—I think you've got to stick to your guns a bit in music and not just follow any trend, because once a fashion comes in, it's already out, if you know what I mean. That's the problem with this funk thing, it's gonna be a fashion or something. It's already in, so that means it's out. I think that funk music deserves a bit more than being a passing fad, you know? It will never get better than that in terms of musicianship and creativity. But I think under the surface there still is a lot to rebel against. Just put on the telly and you'll see that. Keep people sedate, give them everything they want, put mediocre bollocks on the radio and TV, and it keeps everyone on a level where they're not questioning anything.

But if, as you've said, you can only emulate the style and not the same quality of the precursors to the funk movement, why bother?

Because until someone else is doing it really well, then there's always going to be a place for us. I'd love to get a band together doing my [Mo' Wax] stuff, but I can't afford it. I'm having to sell records from my collection to make money. In fairness, I didn't pay much for them and now they're going for mad money, so I don't mind. I'm getting out of that thing where I *have* to have the record—I'd rather find the master tapes and put it out for people to get it for £2 rather than £200. A year ago I would've been sweating over it, like, *Oh, I want that track so bad.* But so what? I might DJ it once a month to a couple of hundred people whereas if you release it off the master tapes you've got thousands who can hear it anytime. Something like this [*holding a copy of the UFOs's "Got a Nice Buzz" on Semp*]—there's so few copies around, who's gonna get to hear it? That's why I don't like that mentality of covering records up, because there's not enough emphasis put on the musicians who made the stuff. Like all that, *I found this record, it's mine. I own it.*

They didn't make it!

Exactly. You've got to be so careful—the people who made it did so at a time where they were fighting everything that's still going on, with the ownership bit. There's a lot of old musicians who made the stuff who're getting ripped off left, right, and center; they're being offered $10 each for records by people who know damn well they can get $500 for it. Some say, "Oh, I'm doing a show at a hospital for some kids and we want to give your records out as prizes. Can you send me a load?" And they send them off. Some of those records are real political, and you don't want to be dragged into abusing that. You're becoming everything they were fucking fighting against.

Is there anything else you want to mention?

One thing I did want to get on to is this thing with crack, because I feel like it's got to be said, really. It's such a dangerous thing; it just sucks your fuckin' insides out. I took it with this Rasta called Papa Love, and that's what saved me, because if I hadn't I would be fucked. Seriously. He just said all the right things, because he'd seen so many people fuck up on it and he'd tried to help them. I used to do it a lot. It throws up two paths: you can be humble on it or you can be bigged up, but you've got to grab for the humble. It's almost religious. To me, the whole God thing is a frame of mind that you can tune into. Your mind is like a radio in that you can tune it into different things, and if you want the bad, you'll fucking get it. But I needed to see that path, otherwise I was gone, mate. It's like something's got a hold of you that is outside yourself, or if it is part of yourself you don't wanna know it—it's like greed and everything that's fucking wrong.

Every one of us is linked in a way we probably won't know for another 1,000 years. I don't know, you're just made to realize that over time. Everything that you do has a knock-on effect; everything that you think, even, has a knock-on effect. Things just come right back around. I've got rare records back when I've pretty much given them away—they've come right back to me. I mean, that makes you think. And if you abuse that…I suppose I suffered the consequences for ignoring that, 'cause things went badly wrong for me. I took the wrong path, you see, in my head. And it just fuckin' collapsed, the whole thing, and I had to question things a bit deeper. But I think I've almost earned a place on the planet. I've got a dark side—God knows I have—but any anger I have I put into the music. ◉

Zaid is a writer from London, where he was born, raised, lives, and now loves and hates in equal measures. After accepting a degree in English Literature from the University of London, he has written for SpineMagazine.com, Breakin' Point, Blues & Soul, Touch, and HipHop.com.

> I THINK I'VE ALMOST EARNED A PLACE ON THE PLANET.

BONGO FLAVA
HIP-HOP IN TANZANIA

by Thomas Gesthuizen

all photos © 1997–1999
Thomas Gesthuizen

Cool Para (left) watches as the Cuttish Crew records the first-ever Zanzibar hip-hop album. *Fun Disco*, 1993.

Merege's first efforts to move to a hip-hop beat seemed a little awkward. But after three weeks of practice, the twenty-four-year-old cow herder from the Serengeti (close to the cradle of mankind) managed to balance his traditional *adumu* jumping dance and singing with the Das EFX-inspired attitude of his crew. Born a Maasai, Merege was never encouraged to tune in to the latest American rap tunes through the airwaves, as his family (and many of the Maasai people of Kenya and Tanzania) chose to live a largely traditional lifestyle away from the city. Still, when he hooked up with the three-member hip-hop crew of X Plastaz who visited his *kraal* (dwelling), he immediately got into the vibe that would lead the group to record an album together and go on tour abroad. For now, this may be the furthest hip-hop can move from the urban settings in which it roots, as even most of Tanzania's hip-hop artists live in the bustling metropolis of Dar es Salaam.

Rapper Abbas from Underground Souls, one of the few Tanzanian crews rapping in English (1999).

The daily DJ show at Clouds FM was immediately popular with the youth (1999).

Hip-hop (and hip-hop culture) has traveled a long way to get to the Serengeti—and has mutated on its way from the Bronx to the back streets of Dar es Salaam. More than ten years into the existence of Tanzanian hip-hop, American rap has passed through pioneering Tanzanian MCs who came up with their own localized flows, topics, and philosophies. Tanzanian MCs subsequently passed the arts on to an audience that might have heard foreign (American) rap before, but wasn't aware of the lyrical content or the full spectrum of hip-hop. The second generation of Tanzanian MCs has created a localized rap music that they named "Bongo flava" (bongo literally meaning brain—but usually referring to the city of Dar es Salaam or the whole of Tanzania), which is quickly becoming the nation's most popular music.

The recent tenfold increase of the number of Tanzanian rap releases seems to run parallel to the rise of hip-hop and R&B on the international market. The new school of MCs would not have made it this far if hip-hop had not been an adaptable art pliable with local circumstances. One of the important tactics was the use of Swahili, which for years was the only language taught at Tanzanian schools and is spoken as a first language by the majority of Tanzanians. The revolutionary politics of *Ujamaa*, or African socialism, in the 1970s did much to create a feeling of national unity and equality, and some of its ethics seem to echo in the local rap lyrics of the new century. But some of the basics of hip-hop culture also fit in with the various traditional cultures of Tanzania. As most hip-hop heads take for a fact, rap music has part of its origins in Africa, and though West Africa's griots (storytellers) are usually mentioned to be early founders, East Africa is also rich in cultural elements that have survived in hip-hop.

DAYS OF THE OLD SCHOOL

Trying to go back to the early days of Tanzanian rap is like digging in a mythical past. Many of the performers and promoters of the late '80s and early '90s have left the game. The remaining stories were rarely documented, so now there exists many different accounts as to who was the first to rhyme in local lingo and what crews rocked in 1993. Very little audio or video recordings of the era exist. Like American rap in the 1970s, Tanzanian rap existed for a decade without much backing by the music industry. Between 1985, when, reportedly, the first local kids took up a mic, and 1995, when the newly introduced commercial radio started out with a regular rap show, only three tapes were made commercially available.

First up was Saleh J's *Ice Ice Baby–King of Swahili Rap*. Saleh J, now living in Abu Dhabi (UAE) with his family, wasn't the first to do Swahili rhymes, nor did he interact much with other kids who were into hip-hop, but his 1992 tape was very successful and influential, as many people realized they could use their native language to spit rhymes. Saleh emerged through "Yo Rap Bonanza," a talent show initiated by a local businessman who helped him get his tape on the market. Saleh's approach was word play and sometimes-literal translations of English rhymes over commercial beats. He was aware of the more hardcore hip-hop too, but the album was built on pop rap instrumentals like "O.P.P.," "The Power," and "Ice Ice Baby," with a remarkably tight Swahili flow on top. "I used to listen to a lot of LL Cool J, Big Daddy Kane, and many others," says Saleh. "You see, what I was doing was only the hits like top ten ones in the States. I knew people would like them."

In 1993, Kwanza Unit, a Wu-Tang-sized crew comprised of members of other early rap groups, released the first album with self-produced beats to get radio play. They were in touch with fam abroad to send them the latest underground hip-hop tapes, and thus Gang Starr, Big Daddy Kane, and NWA became major influences. Their beats were constructed by Bonnie Luv, a DJ who would spin at the popular rap and R&B club Mawingu on the weekends. Their lyrics combined the strong messages to society—partly rooted in African socialism—with topics that were inspired by American examples.

Mambo Poa, a group mixing Caribbean zouk with rap, at a rap competition. As usual, the crowd is seated around the dancefloor (2000). — Abdulli (right) and Cool Para at Fuji, Zanzibar's legendary club where local hip-hop originates. — Gangsters with Matatizo, a group that popularized the use of Swahili slang in rap (1999).

Tanzania was undergoing major economic changes when, in 1995, TV broadcasting was introduced and commercial radio was allowed to develop. A wealthy businessman started ITV and Radio One, which had a weekly local rap show that reached a wider audience, and subsequently the Radio One studios became flooded with demos. One of the new discoveries was an MC called 2 Proud (or Mr II as he calls himself now), whose streetwise Swahili lyrics did well on the radio. "Ndani ya Bongo," a posse track from his second album, became an anthem with its use of Swahili slang to promote pride in the emerging urban culture. Though Tanzania doesn't have the income or status hierarchy of other developing countries, it is one of the poorest countries in Africa. Education and work prospects for the youth haven't been very promising for decades, and 2 Proud's conscious lyrics focused on this situation. The political criticism of some of 2 Proud's songs caught on with the radio listeners, and soon his name was familiar even with kids in the smallest countryside villages.

MUSIC INDUSTRY

Economic decline and music piracy had reduced efforts to set up labels releasing Tanzanian music, and by the mid-'90s, a network of Indian businessmen controlled what cassettes were released. Gradually, cover designs and sound quality improved, and by 1999, some groups were able to get better deals with the distributors (the former pirates who had built up a large distribution network as far as Zambia). Radio was playing much more foreign rap and R&B, and when Clouds Entertainment launched a station, the city of Dar es Salaam was up-to-date with the American billboard. At this time, underground hip-hop was played weekly on more than three stations.

With thousands of young people facing the realities of unemployment and overpopulation, many in today's free-market Tanzania immediately seize a good idea. MCs sharpened their skills in all corners of the city, awaiting an opportunity to surface. In the last four years, the older generation of Tanzanians has started to accept hip-hop, no longer considering it to be *uhuni* (criminal), but respecting rap as a medium to bring out positive messages to the youth. Some established older musicians became involved with rap, like singer/band leader King Kiki, whose song "Msafiri" was sampled by Kwanza Unit, and the rebellious singer Remmy Ongala, who participated in a rap song about HIV.

At this point, commerce came on board: beer and cigarette companies set up rap competitions; Clouds FM started a music promotion agency, which managed to elevate the fame of rap and R&B singers; and NGOs hired MCs to translate their slogans to the youth. Many MCs realized that they had a new chance of securing a distribution deal, especially after the hugely successful releases of the latest Hardblasters album (one of the pioneering groups) and Gangwe Mobb singles. Suddenly, everyone wanted to record a single for radio promotion, and the studios soon became overbooked.

A couple of pioneering hip-hop studios, most notably those of talented producers Master J and P-Funk, did some heavy upgrading over the past three years and are now banging out tracks on a daily basis. Initially, their beats depended on sampled loops, as Master J had a good collection of old jazz and funk records. Though this method has defined the particular sound of Tanzanian production, producers have now resorted to using sound modules or cut-up samples, and since 2001, to sampling traditional music. Master J and P-funk hired other producers to work in their studios, such as Ludigo and Raja Master. Other players in the local production field became visible, including the well-respected Finnish producer Miika Mwamba (FM Studio), while DJ Bonnie Luv reinstated the defunct Mawingu studio. The new Tanzanian production sound is now so sophisticated that MCs from neighboring countries have preferred to make the trip to Dar es Salaam to record their albums.

X Plastaz, Achompong Clan, and Hardcore Unit all share the rugged and no-compromise attitude that characterizes the hip-hop from Arusha city (1999).

Ziggy of X Plastaz in front of barbershop sporting his namesake (Arusha, 1999).

Cool Para at an East German housing project built during the days of African socialism (Zanzibar, 2006).

BONGO FLAVA ON THE INTERNATIONAL LEVEL

Considering the current boom in production and investment in local rap music, one would think that Tanzania's hip-hop scene could produce a number of crews that are able to live off their music and gain international success. On the African continent, only Senegal, South Africa, and Ghana have enjoyed a degree of foreign attention to their hip-hop scene. Dar es Salaam can easily be compared to Dakar for the number of MCs and quality of the music, but it isn't as well connected as Senegal, which "enjoys" French post-colonial ties and often sees its artists going overseas to tour and record albums. Still, a number of Tanzanian MCs have raised heads outside of East Africa. Mr II has been traveling since 1998, and recorded his third album, *Nje ya Bongo*, in Amsterdam with producer Mongo Star. Other trips led him to perform at the WOMEX trade fair in Sweden, in Texas for the large Tanzanian community, and at Holland's Festival Mundial where he was joined by Dola Soul, the X Plastaz, and Fortune Tellers.

Tanzanian hip-hop developed without much interaction with other African countries. But as Swahili is also spoken in Uganda, Kenya, Rwanda, and Burundi, the potential market for Tanzanian rappers is vast (an estimated forty to fifty million Swahili speakers worldwide; even Chuck D and Flava Flav took Swahili classes in the 1970s). The Dar es Salaam-based East Africa FM recently started broadcasting in three East African capitals, and within weeks the hip-hop show became hugely popular, with Tanzanian tracks climbing up the Kenyan and Ugandan charts. There have been some collaborations between Kenyan and Tanzanian rappers, such as "Tunajirusha," a party track which brought together the popular duo of Gangwe Mobb with Kenyan female MC Nazizi and her crew. Kalamashaka, a popular Kenyan group, recorded their full album in P-Funk's Tanzanian studio and hooked up with many local crews.

NODES IN THE INTERNATIONAL HIP-HOP NETWORK

Since the old school days, when few Tanzanians could get hold of the latest American hip-hop releases, gear, and info, the metropolis of Dar es Salaam has been a node in the spread of hip-hop culture. This is where the local rap pioneers lived, some of who attended international schools or were part of a circle of diplomats' and ministers' sons. In a country where the majority of the population has a very limited understanding of English, hip-hop's core concepts and expressions had to be translated by these early exponents. The first Swahili rap releases relied on the artist's sole interpretation, where curses and references to sexuality were left out in accordance with local culture. The use of slang, the emphasis on street knowledge and knowledge of self, and a critical attitude towards oppression, abuse of political power, and neo-colonialism were integrated into Tanzanian hip-hop.

In other Tanzanian cities, local hip-hop scenes developed under the influence of the Dar es Salaam styles as much as any other music. The city of Arusha, surrounded by the Maasai Steppe, hosts a scene that never needed to adapt itself to the demands of radio, TV, and competitions. Consequently, the rap styles, dress, and topics were much more rugged than those of Dar es Salaam. The X Plastaz—three brothers who worked in a barbershop—made a name on the local scene with their Das EFX-influenced "sewa style" rap. They were very critical of the performance and lyrics of MCs from Dar and chose to develop a unique style in which they fused other Tanzanian languages and music. The topics they rapped about related to the ghetto environment they grew up in, striking a chord with the local youth. A pirated cassette containing their track "Bamiza" (recorded live in 1997 over Akinyele's "Fuck Me for Free" beat) sold all the way down to South Africa. They teamed up with Maasai singer Merege and their rapping brother and sister (ages twelve and fourteen), and in June 2001, the crew was invited to tour Europe, record their first full album, and shoot a music video.

Mr II (left) and Dola Soul in the inner city of Dar es Salaam.

Mr II (right) and Dola Soul performing live at Festival Mundial in Holland (June 2001).

Many MCs dream of a career leading up to a tour abroad, but some others have focused on their local audience. The island of Zanzibar for example, with its centuries-old traditions and tight Muslim community, hosts a new phenomenon called "taa-rap." Local MC, Cool Para, one of the island's popular wedding and club DJs, managed to bridge the gap between a non-hip-hop audience and the kids watching foreign music videos. His lyrics are composed in a way reminiscent of traditional Swahili poetry, while his beats are created by *taarab* musicians. Taarab, a genre carrying elements of Arabic, Indian, and indigenous African music, is extremely popular with people from the East African coast. Taarab lyrics are filled with metaphors saying what can't otherwise be said in a conservative society. One of taarab's top groups, East African Melody, provides Cool Para's instrumental tracks, while a popular singer is brought in to sing the chorus (often "sampling" from her own previous hit song), after which the rapper drops his verses. This fusion has now been picked up in the mainland by groups like Gangwe Mobb, who carried it to the national level by revamping the taarab classic "Vidonge," a song especially popular among Swahili women.

With an army of hype MCs lined up, plus an increasing pride in local hip-hop, top range recording studios, and a number of music videos being made, Tanzania seems destined to join the international network of hip-hop-producing countries. The Internet has already facilitated some of this, as most MCs have opened up email accounts and are visiting forums and chat rooms of international sites. Budding producers have been downloading cracked versions of music recording software, opening up no-budget studios and producing music with Acid, Reason, and Fruityloops audio programs. Some crews have created their own websites offering new tracks.

Presently, the Internet is the best way to hear Bongo flava, as most tapes can only be obtained in Tanzania. Even locally cassettes are rare, as most are sold in a one-off pressing of between 500 and 3,000 copies—popular titles like Mr II's *Nje ya Bongo* might get multiple reprints. So far, no Tanzanian albums have been released on the international market (though X Plastaz's *Ushanta* will be released in 2002). Recently, recording artists have been saving their songs to CD-R, and, subsequently, pirated CD compilations have started to surface. Despite such piracy, the new digital medium provides a chance for the music to live on in posterity. Unfortunately, the early classics of the 1990s were mastered onto cheap ferro cassette tapes, most MCs have long since lost their copies, and frugal studios used tapes multiple times, so there are few spots where history was preserved. ○

THOMAS GESTHUIZEN *lives in Amsterdam, Holland, and is editor-in-chief of AfricanHipHop.com. He is involved with Madunia, a non-profit organization that promotes African hip-hop and urban culture, and researches the role of rap as a medium of communication.*

Cool Muza on the mic with DJ Cool Para behind the decks (Zanzibar, 1998).

Abbas (left) and Kwanza Unit MC, KBC, who ran a popular urban music show at Clouds FM in Dar es Salaam (1999).

Producer P-Funk (right) with rapper Saigon in his first studio set-up (1997).

MWAKA ELFU MBILI
HIP HOP EVENT

performances of tanzania's best hip hop crews

featuring:
Deplowmatz
G.W.M.
Unique Sisters
Gangwe Mob
2 Proud
KBC (Kwanza Unit)
Underground Souls
dj P-Funk (Halfani)

special guests:
X PLASTAZ 'BAMIZA' (Arusha)
Fortune Tellers
(youngest rappers in TZ)

other groups to be announced – stay tuned to Clouds FM and Radio 1

SUNDAY 9 MAY, 1999
FROM 14.00 TO 20.00
FM CLUB, KINONDONI
ENTRANCE TSH 500 ONLY

poster design: rumba-kuli productions (rumba-kuli@eudoramail.com)

Poster for a hip-hop festival in a dancehall (Dar es Salaam, 1999).

COMMON GROUND

by Cosmo Baker – photos by Bryan Hitch

A big DO NOT ENTER sign graces the front door of Val Shively's R&B Records. First-time customers have stood confused in front of that door in the freezing Philly winter air, not bothering to read the sign a little closer—handwritten in Magic Marker, it reads, "unless you know what you want."

But anyone can see the huge sign on his roof that reads "Over 4,000,000 oldies in stock"; it's unmistakable when you're driving around Upper Darby, right outside of West Philadelphia. The first time I mustered up the courage to enter the store, I thought back to warnings of how the proprietors could "make you feel like you don't know anything." That's kind of how it is, though. When you walk in through that front door, you are living in their world, playing by their rules. But, oh, what a world it is.

I had wanted to replace a record that had "mysteriously disappeared" after a gig in Las Vegas. Intent on getting another copy, I walked in, and, immediately, stacks and stacks of 12-inch vinyl surrounded me. Above the stacks of wax were walls that had old 8 × 10 glossy photos of bands I've never heard of, and gold records for songs that I didn't know existed. There was a counter that separated the front part of the store from the unbelievable rows of 7-inch wax in the back. Two guys were concentrating on pulling records from the walls and a third guy was talking on the phone, calling for records from the other two while trying to take notes and sort small stacks of 45s. The man, an average looking white guy in his mid-fifties, looks up at me with a cold gaze and says, "What do you need?"

I felt as though my very presence in their store was fucking up their program, so I, not one to make waves at all, humbly cleared my throat. "Um, do you have Freddie Scott's 'You Got What I Need' on 45?" Without even batting an eye he calls back, "Chuck? John? Would one of you guys pull Freddie Scott? He's on the Shout label"—and goes right back to his phone call. They found it, I got it and was gone, but that was it for me. I knew that I was hooked. And by the way Val looked at me as I left, he knew that I would be back. That was years ago.

I started coming back on the regular. I've been a 45 hound for almost as long as I've been DJing, which is well over ten years, yet funk 45s—at least the real choice ones—never really made themselves available. So now I decided it was time to catch up on all that I had missed. My first goal was to replace all the songs that I had been playing out as a DJ on LP or 12-inch to 45. I've been doing this for way too long. I have bad legs and knees, and I don't feel like carrying these damn crates anymore. Plus, to be honest with you, it just looks so damn cool. My second goal was to grab all the records that I knew about but didn't have. These guys seemed to really know their music, so I figured that I'd start coming in with my want lists. The third goal, one that I never thought that I would be in a position to follow through with, was to get behind that counter and start getting my hands dirty in those immense piles of records, just looking for something, anything, everything.

I became a fixture around the shop to a degree. Customers were usually looking for one or two oldies: a Flamingos

here, a Heartbeats there. I would watch as many a mobile DJ would come in and get records for weddings and anniversaries. Occasionally there would be the obvious beathead asking for particular records, or some odd British cat with a laundry list of northern soul. I always wondered how in the hell they could keep track of anything. Val's desk is covered with a thousand little slips of paper, various 45s, and half-full soda bottles. He wouldn't have it any other way though, as it's a perfect organizational technique for him. He knows where everything is in a New York minute. This self-proclaimed control freak needs to always have his hands on every part of the business. I eventually learned that all the records on the shelves were sorted by label. If you didn't know what label the record you were looking for was on, it made the search for it that much tougher, no matter what other information you had on it.

I went up to Val's a couple of days after 9/11. I had stressed myself over the whole situation, especially since I spent the entire first day trying to get in contact with my brother, an NYU film student. One thing that calms me down and helps me forget my troubles is digging through old stacks of records, and I figured that Val's was the perfect place to partake in such meditation. Everybody was out of it that week, including Val, who I could see was visibly distracted when I walked in the store. With the lack of business, and the innate need for communication that the situation instilled in everyone at that time, we got to rapping. Under the stern gaze of his steely eyes there was a hell of a lot more to this man.

Val Shively grew up with stern parents in the Upper Darby neighborhood of Philadelphia, a working class neighborhood in the '50s. "Since I can remember, music was the thing," he says. "I started buying pop records in 1956, mostly listening to white pop stations like WIBG, which was the big station in this town. Everybody listened to that. When I heard something that I liked, like Bobby Darin's 'Splish Splash,' which came out in 1957…I would wait for them to come off of the jukeboxes. It would cost a dollar [for a new] record, which was a lot of money for me, especially back then.…I knew where all the jukebox operators were, so I would wait until the records were dead and get them five for a dollar." Val bought up Bobby Darin records, Chuck Berry, Little Richard—"anything that was popular on the radio at the time," he says. "I started buying records like there was no tomorrow." Right then and there, all other hobbies went by the wayside.

"Pretty soon I had thousands and thousands of records, and I was into every aspect of collecting records. The groups, the labels, everything." He made the fledgling steps of his now-empire by selling the extra copies of the records that he amassed to his schoolmates. "Around 1959, I decided to curb my record buying by getting a reel-to-reel tape recorder and taping music from my transistor radio. I used to carry this big old transistor around with me all the time. Around the same time, I started to fool with the dial and see what was happening. I said to myself, *I wonder what's going on all the way to the right of the dial?* Black radio, which was relegated to the far end of the radio

wave spectrum, was what he found. "It blew my mind!" he remembers. "The music was far superior. So I spent the entire year of 1960 inside taping songs off the radio, effectively ruining any chance of having a social life.

"I graduated high school in 1961 and started attending Pierce Business School in downtown Philly. All the while I was still raiding the jukebox joints and selling records to kids I knew. But money wasn't the point of me doing it. I just wanted to have the best collection. I loved music, so I wanted to make sure that I had the records that were important to me in my collection." In 1962, a classmate suggested he tune into WCAM, a small radio station that was broadcasted out of Camden, New Jersey, to hear Jerry "the Geator with the Heator" Blavat's show. The Geator was a wild radio broadcaster who modeled his show and on-air antics after legendary radio broadcasters like Philly's Jocko Henderson from WHAT and WDAS AM. Jocko actually got his act from the radio DJ "Hot Rod," who broadcasted out of Baltimore, MD, and who is generally considered, by old school heads, as the first rhymer.

"The first night I tuned into the station I was disappointed," Val tells me. "Here was all this Latin crap. Then the kid told me, 'No, you have to tune in late night'—so I did. When I finally heard it, I was like, *What the hell is this?* I mean, I thought I knew shit. I had tons of records, more than anybody, and now all of the sudden I'm hearing records that made me say, *What is this music?* This changed my whole idea of things. So all the old pop records were done, and *this* was the music that I needed to have. The sound of Black vocal groups really was cemented as the sound of choice for me. The harmonies, the bass, the high notes, all of it."

"So this kid from my class joined me on my quest around the neighborhoods of Philadelphia in search of independent R&B records. We were going downtown to buy some record sleeves one day, and on the way back the kid saw a five-and-dime that had a sign in the window, '3 records for a dollar.' So you know how that is, especially when your mind is always on the lookout for records. We went racing to get to the crates and start to scour through them." In these crates of wax Val found two of his most wanted records at the time: "Footstomping Pt.1" by the Flares on Felsted and "Just a Lonely Christmas" by the Moonglows on Chance—red vinyl—written by the famous Harvey Fuqua.

Later they passed the Record Museum, a legendary store at 10th and Market Street, which is to this day Philly's best area to get the latest hip-hop and breakbeat records. "It was a Saturday afternoon and the place was packed with kids raising a ruckus," he remembers. "They were mostly kids around my age and younger, and [on] the walls were lists and lists of records that they were offering money for. Now I thought of myself as Mister Records, and I'm looking over these lists, and I couldn't find almost any title that I recognized." But he did recognize one: the Moonglows—and the Record Museum was offering $12 for it.

"So I said to the guy behind the counter, 'Hey, mister, I got that record.' The guy said to me, 'Yeah? You're full of shit.'" As Val argued with the clerk, who would only give $12 in credit or $6 in cash, someone kicked him from behind. The guy pulls him to the side and says, "I'll give you $10 for that record. Meet me outside in five minutes." Eager to do so, he went outside and completed the sale, elated at the profit margin. Val seemed to feel the adrenaline rush all over again as he told the story.

Six months later he found out that Philadelphia was "nothing" and that all the activity—"insane craziness" as he calls it—was coming out of a store in New York called Times Square Records. TSR was owned by Irving "Slim" Rose and was located inside a NYC subway station at 42nd and Broadway. "They used to hold all the records on the wall with tape because when the trains rolled by the whole place would shake and they would come falling on the floor." He had no money, but had an incredible drive to obtain new R&B records. Eighteen-year-old Val sold his 3,000 records for ten cents apiece to buy these new records. He got on a bus and made the pilgrimage to Times Square and was amazed with how much more music they had. "Here were all these kids, just like in Philly but much more, and they're all packed in the store shouting out for records and writing down the names of the groups and the titles of the songs. It was a real madhouse. In all this madness, some guy looks at me and says, 'You look familiar.'

Me, well, I puff out my chest and say, 'I don't think so, man, I'm from Philly!'

"And the guy says, 'That's it! Hey, Slim, here's the asshole from Philly that sold me the [Moonglows] record.'" After he had bought it off Val for $10, he went back into the Record Museum and traded it for $200 in records.

Val spent the rest of his time at Times Square Records writing down the names and labels of these great records and went back to Philly, where he branched out to North and West Philly, all the way down to Chester and even over to Camden to find these records. Vinyl fever had infected his bloodstream.

Just as he begun to rebuild his collection with strictly the choicest R&B records of the early '60s, he moved to Kentucky with his family. Val was being taken away from his friends and his music. "For what?" he asks. "To watch the corn?" But he moved, got a job as an accountant, and became a recluse, shut away from his passion for the world of music. After a year of scrimping and saving, Val made his escape back to Philly. On his arrival, he was greeted with the rude awakening of a changed world. The climate had changed from people being enraptured by the sweet serenades of the street corner symphonies to that of Beatlemania.

Val eventually got a job with wholesale distributor Norman Cooper, who bought all his records from Henry Stone's Tone Distributors out of Florida—home of the Alston, Marlin, Rockin, Cat, and TK imprints, and whose warehouse workers included Harry Wayne Casey, later of KC & the Sunshine Band. Cooper serviced most of the Philadelphia area. Val went from delivering all the latest hits to spots all around Funky North Philly—while doing his own searching and collecting of the finest in independent R&B and soul records—to handling all the duties of working at Cooper's one-stop, from buying the records and keeping the books to hiring help.

Val hired on a young saxophone player as a favor to a client. During his lunch hour, the kid would practice on his sax in lieu of eating. "We would tell him, 'Hey, man, don't play that shit, we're trying to eat; you're gonna make us throw up!'" Val remembers treating everything as a big joke. A year later, Val's hired-hand, a one Grover Washington, Jr., got the opportunity to be a KUDU session player on Johnny Hammond's *Breakout*. Not long afterward, Washington was hired back for another session—but Hammond got arrested in Tennessee for drunk driving. Not to let the studio time go to waste, they recorded material for Washington—yielding the 1971 hit *Inner City Blues*. Washington worked with Val for about another year before he was able to make a good living on his music.

I sit in amazement of the stories from these long-forgotten times. I sit in awe of this character, and that's in the truest sense of the word "character." A couple of weeks ago Val slipped and broke a bone in his vertebrae. Against the urges of his doctor and his wife to stay in bed and recuperate, he's here in the store wrapping packages, stacking records and holding court for me and about five other people who came to shop and got wrapped up in these stories. It's mesmerizing to watch him move and gesture with his hands as he speaks. "I never thought that I'd work for myself, I always thought that I'd work for [Norman Cooper]," Val tells me.

"The summer of 1972, I went to see my mom down south. I was with this kid from London, who I liked. So I said that he should come with me and maybe we would look for some records." Val and his British friend go to Nashville, all the while his friend nagging that "there's nothing in Nashville." The two end up at a store called Buckley's, which is filled with 78s. "I hate 78s," Val says. As his friend looks through the 78s, Val finds out that the upstairs holds vinyl. The manager tells Val that nobody has ever been upstairs. "I say, 'What's the price?' and she says, 'Whatever you want to pay. Just don't fall through the ceiling.' So I go upstairs—*tons of records*…records that are legendary. And I'm shaking." When the woman tried to interrupt Val's search—because she had to go home—Val promised her a steak dinner and a ride home to let them stay. "The whole car was full of records. I remember [driving] her home, we stuffed her in someplace!"

Upon his return he found his workplace to be in such disarray that he finally decided to quit and open up his own shop. The mother lode of records that he had just found in Nashville helped bolster his collection enough so it was

finally possible. "I did it for the first six months out of my house, which I thought would be cool. I figured that I could do mail order; I wouldn't have to pay no [store] rent. What do I need a store for? But two things happened. Number one was I never got dressed, I never shaved. I became a recluse. Working in my underwear, I don't have to do shit! So I started to lose sight of the world. And number two was some very shaky people started to come to my house. And my collection is up there, and that's what's really sacred to me—my record collection.

"My goal from the beginning was to have the best record collection. It's not about money. Once I started with the mail order thing I became pretty big with this. If you wanted old records, I was the guy." Around 1971, the old R&B scene exploded in New York. "The only problem," Val tells me, "was that no record shops carried this shit. See it's all timing. This is all happening around the same time. All of the sudden I'm getting busloads of kids in from New York coming to see me here in Philadelphia. It's like what I used to do was now happening to me. There were two other guys in California. Their names were Henry and Art Mariano out of San Mateo. We were the game.

"I used to put out these mailing lists every now and then with what I had, what I would sell it for, and on the back what I was looking for. Now there was a guy from Detroit who interviewed me for a newspaper but the article never came out. A couple of months later I went on a cruise with my now-wife, and the Mariano brothers and their dates, and when I came back there was no mail in my post office box. The people at the post office pulled me into the back and showed me my mail. It was stacks and stacks and stacks up to the ceiling. I used to get maybe ten–fifteen letters a week.

The reporter had sold the article to the *National Inquirer* (1975). "Old records are worth big money," it said. Val remembers reading, "'Everybody's probably got them in their basement. If you want to know what your records are worth, this guy [Val] makes millions of dollars.' It [was] all bullshit! It scared the shit out of me! Man, I thought I was going to jail." Val hired people to sort through the letters and do mail-outs. "My catalogs were free at first. It cost me a buck to make it. I didn't give a shit if you were gonna buy something or not. You might have something…I'm looking for. So all these letters are people that wanted catalogs. I ended up getting a half a million letters [from] people with records, and I sent out probably 100,000 catalogs. So I did really unbelievably, and I've never had to do another catalog since," Val says.

"When I first started the store in 1972, it was going to be just what I loved, the vocal harmony groups. Then I thought that I should carry all the other stuff, funk, different stuff, so it just started growing. I've made some insane deals with radio stations, jukebox distributors for everything. This guy came by one day with a dumptruck with the back filled with dirt and…records. The records were just shoveled in. A store in West Philly collapsed…and they just shoveled [the records] into the truck with the mortar and plaster and glass. All that shit was all funk, all that stuff that people are killing for today. See, back then it meant nothing, but now it's something. That's the way it is. Lawrence Welk could kick off tomorrow for all I know. I've seen it all," he says.

"I love all that oddball shit that nobody pays attention to. I pride myself by making a living off of the industry's mistakes. See, about all that funk stuff, when I see kids coming in—and, see, first of all it's a young thing, you guys are keeping it going. Just like I keep it going in my own world. You know what, young people, the funk, it's exciting to me. It's not where my head is, but you know what, I can appreciate it 'cause it's the same deal that I'm into. The same thing, just off-the-wall, oddball shit that nobody paid any attention to. And you guys are making something out of it."

At this point it was dark outside, and I could tell that Val was feeling the effects of such an animated conversation. I decided that I would wrap things up and get on the road. I had a show to do that night anyway so I handed my stack of 45s to Val. He thumbed through them: the Nu-Sound Express, "Ain't It Good Enough" on Silver Dollar; the Parliaments, "Good Old Music" on Revilot; Isley Brothers, "Keep on Doing" on T Neck; Syl Johnson, "Is It Because I'm Black" on Twinight; Minnie Ripperton, "Adventures in Paradise" on Epic; and gave me my price. It was a reasonable price, Val being very fair with me. You see, Val knows what he has; he's no fool. And he knows what he can get for the records that he sells. But he also knows that the value of these records is much more than any price that can be put on a piece of plastic. What he's selling is his passion, his memories and a view into his soul. It's funny how much we have in common. We both share a passion on the verge of madness. But it's a beautiful thang. Like he said to me before, "It's all about the music." A love for this old music—from a buck like me to an OG like Val—is truly the greatest common ground that there is. ●

COSMO BAKER, *a Philly-based DJ/producer/promoter, wrote the "Digging in the Crates" article for* On the Go *magazine back in the early '90s.*

CUTTING CORNERS

by Dante Carfagna

fig. 1

fig. 2

fig. 3

fig. 4

Any collector who has seen any time in the bins will be familiar with the LP that seems to be missing something. An indiscriminate triangle, a desultory circle, or perhaps an all but invisible round vacuity are present. Ah, but the vinyl's clean, and said LP is purchased. As days in the bin turn to years in the racks, we begin to take notice that all of the LPs we picked up and have never, or rarely, seen again have this partial material absence. We learn that these (un)markings are known as the cut-out mark, and are used to signify those releases that have been discounted or have been allotted for promotional use. We also observe that the cut-out takes many shapes and forms, from glaringly obvious to barely noticeable. Here we will make a small taxonomic journey into the nature of the cut-out.

The most commonly occurring form the cut-out takes will be called the *standard cut corner* [*fig.1*], as this rendering has been used by almost all record labels, large or small. Generally, the cut-out, and in particular the standard cut corner, was used to designate titles that weren't selling particularly well in the first run record outlets and had been discounted in an effort to move the surplus stock. There are many US titles that seem to be found *only* as cut-outs, and more often than not these titles have found their way into collectability. Many European titles that were picked up for small US distribution by large US labels are invariably designated as non-sellers by the cut corner. Apparently Can, Captain Beefheart, and other improvisational rock groups were a hard sell to the hegemonic pop record buyers, as they went almost directly to the cheapo bins at the discount department store. This assignment brings up an interesting socio-economic theory, as lower income record buyers could more easily afford seemingly "strange" records by unknown groups, the musico-cosmos of the plebian LP collector would vary greatly from the standard retail price quo. Witness formation of cult groups.

The cut corner has two variations from the standard, these we will call the *polite cut corner* [*fig. 2*] and the *obnoxious cut corner* [*fig. 3*]. The polite cut corner is a smaller mark, hardly distracting from the appearance of the cover art. In many cases, an argument could be made as to whether or not this was actually a cut-out with a "Naw, that's just a ding on the corner." Differing greatly from the microscopy of the polite, the obnoxious cut corner is impossible to miss. There are many degrees to this example, from slightly larger than the standard cut corner to absolutely ruining the cover art in it's enormity. I once saw a copy of Ralph McDonald *Sound of a Drum* on Marlin in which half of the cover had been removed in an effort to *really* designate the fact that it was discounted. Now this example *truly* should have been cheaper, for there was a significant amount of actual material missing from the object. Had the record been in the jacket, it would have been cut in two, which brings to light that this LP was cut-out initially *from the label* and was made to be sold cheaply from square one. Did Bambaataa jam on the groove at full retail? Or buy doubles out of the cut-out bin?

In the same family, though certainly a different species of cut corner, is the *rounded cut corner* [*fig. 4*]. This mark tends to appear on records from the mid-'70s onwards, and is really common in cut-outs from the '80s. The rounded cut corner was usually implemented by slightly smaller labels, perhaps as a way to distinguish their loss leaders from those of the corporate failures. It would also appear that this method of discounting was actually spot on, for very few of the rounded cut corners I have seen have actually warranted purchase, even at the knockdown price. Though as time rolls on, perhaps these titles will also become cut-out musical landmarks on par with the Skip Spences and Linda Perhacs of the world. Prediction: severe Homestead label rarities.

Though not quite as widespread as the cut corner, the *standard saw-mark* [*fig. 5*] is also a commonly used discount indicator. The saw-mark is usually found on the spine side of the LP jacket, either at the top or the bottom, and is usually about an inch long. Forever will the tight-shelved collector moan about the pitfalls of the longer saw-mark, for as they try to slip their prized James Knight and the Butlers LP between Curtis and Jean, the saw-mark acts as perforation/score and the isolated cardboard between mark and the edge of the jacket folds. Downgrade cover to VG++.

fig. 5

The standard saw-mark also has a cousin, referred to here as the *quick saw-mark* [*fig. 6*]. This mark is much smaller than the norm, as if the person performing the cardboard carpentry realized he needed to make smaller and quicker cuts if he was to really finish cutting out all ten thousand copies of the Insect Trust on Atco before the whistle at 5:00. The saw-mark in all it's forms has seen itself popular throughout the recorded age, even lending itself to changes in format, as witnessed on the 8-track and the compact disc.

fig. 6

Our next cut-out form is one of many clothes and personalities: the punch hole. We will begin with the *common punch hole* [*fig. 7*], which is usually a little smaller than a dime and located in the upper right hand corner of the LP. The common punch hole is frequently used to nominate releases as promotional copies for the industry, but is sometimes employed to indicate remainders or price-reductions. Capitol Records, normally not known for reducing the price of non-selling titles (they had a reasonable return policy, resulting in subsequent recycling of cardboard and vinyl), often effected the common punch hole for its few cut-outs. (Capitol's myriad of cut-out techniques will be dealt with in the coming paragraphs.) The common punch hole had its detractors, "Man, that hole made a hole in the lyric sheet, and I can't read what the last lyric of 'Sinking of the Titanic' is"; yet it also had its proponents, "Check it out, Steve, I can hang my copy of *Fragile* on this nail." It is routine to find the common punch hole used to cut-out gatefold covers, more so than say, the cut corner.

fig. 7

A tasteful and unassuming variant of the common punch hole is the *small punch hole* [*fig. 8*]. This version can be located in any of the four corners of the LP jacket, though usually found in the same region as the common punch hole. This cut-out tactic was enforced by most labels, from Reprise to Sackville to Mbari, and may be the most economic way of designating remainders or discounts. And it could still be hung on a nail. There are times that the small punch hole can become exceedingly belligerent, as shown by the *sloppy small punch hole* [*fig. 9*]. This occurs when the drill used to make the mark was moving too slow or simply couldn't quite get through the fifty-count box of Hollins and Starr LPs. This aberration of the cover art might also be blamed on the same drill-press engineer who was hurrying to complete the earlier Atco job. So many cut-outs, so short a lunch break.

fig. 8

Perhaps the most unassuming, sometimes downright invisible, modification of the punch hole is the ubiquitous *bb hole* [*fig. 10*]. This obviously has nothing to do with BB guns, but as the gauge of the drill bit used to mark the LP is so slim, it actually does resemble the perforation that a BB gun might make if shot into an LP. The bb hole is almost always found in the middle of the LP jacket, for its real purpose was not to distinguish the cover, but rather to puncture the label on the actual record. This method was the only physical cut-out technique used to discount 45s, as the label was

fig. 9

fig. 10

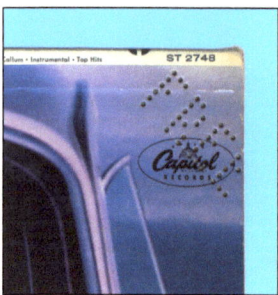

fig. 11

the only non-precious material able to be manipulated on a single. Many collectors will also be aware of the strange by-product of the 45 bb hole, a small volcano-like build up of dead vinyl that sticks up a few millimeters off the label. This was to be found on singles at the bottom of the batch to be cut-out, as the drill heated up due to work, when it was pulled back through it left the actual drilled-out wax on the bottom copy in the box. This black vinyl ring can also be found on LPs cut out with the bb hole technique. This waxy build-up can usually be picked off, and so far I have never met any persons who collect vinyl volcanoes removed from rare records. The Chess family of labels is notorious for having the highest bb hole refuse ratio, with Cadet being the crown champion.

As we survey the cut-out and its many costumes, one may wonder why the record companies chose to actually disfigure the LP rather than designate it with a simple sticker or stamp. For this question, we can offer many explanations, all of which would have pros and cons. The promo record is commonly found, with no cut-out marks, with a promo sticker or rubber stamp, yet the discounted LP rarely has an adhesive attachment claiming "Cheap" or "Couldn't sell this one." This may be due to the label trying to discreetly place titles on the budget market without affecting the artist's composure, or more likely because it would be easy for the shady retailer to remove a sticker and attempt to return a discounted record for its full list price.

The Capitol label, one of the largest record companies in the US, had some unique distinguishing marks for their promotional LPs. They had a FREE or PROMO stamped diagonally into the upper right corner in a weird pointillist font [*fig. 11*]. Due to the size of the Capitol operation, there are many tragically obscure and excellent records that simply disappeared upon release (especially during the late-'60s "green label" era), and if found, usually hold the promo stamp on their covers. Yet Capitol did little remaindering, instead they chose to recycle a large portion of non-selling titles. Thus, outside of the limited promo copies, the only extant copies are the ones that the adventurous record buyer has held on to. And like most obscure titles that were actually good, the copies are now absolutely hammered due to heavy play and the inability to find a replacement copy. Gandalf and David Axelrod are obvious examples of this procedure.

In any circumstance, the cut-out record bin housed what is becoming the true museum of recorded aural evolution. Talk of "ahead of its time" or "too far out" is commonly bantered when discussing records, almost always with saw-marks, that found their audience twenty-five years too late. Much of the break-collecting cadre are full-time cut-out bin devotees, whether they are aware of it or not. I have never met an older music fan, even a hardcore one, that can claim they "really jammed that Brethren LP" or that "Power of Zeus was my joint," yet legions of twenty-something music collectors treat both of these bands like old hats. Hats with breaks for sure, and a new canon is established. The break as *invitation to the world of recorded sound* should not be overlooked. I have met scores of individuals who began looking for records simply for the prospect of finding an unknown open break, and ended up really enjoying the music of AB Skhy or the Incredible String Band. Their pursuits soon took a turn toward simply uncovering obscure music in general, break or no break. And anytime they find an LP they really really feel, private press or major label, it usually has that omnipresent cut-out mark. ●

A graduate from the Kansas City Art Institute with a degree in painting, DANTE CARFAGNA *can never have too many private press LPs, and collects anything with a likeness to an owl.*

re:Discovery

Ike Turner and the Kings of Rhythm *A Black Man's Soul* (Pompeii, 1969)

by J. P. Jones

Teenage Chess Records A&R man. One of the chief architects of the Baby Fetus they call rock 'n' roll. Fifty percent of one of popular music's greatest and most successful duos. Writer of bona fide hits. Is there any credible rock 'n' roll history book in existence that doesn't detail the highlights of Ike Turner's contributions?

Considering the storm this man has endured over his seventy years, he has persevered and without question positively rehabilitated his life and career. (Ike's latest album, *Here and Now*, was nominated for a 2002 Best Blues Instrumental Grammy.) The seemingly inexhaustible Ike also continues playing his lion's share of shows throughout the world. With a new album on the horizon, Ike's story is clearly far from over.

A Black Man's Soul, released in 1969, is unarguably at the top of his long list of fine achievements, an underappreciated, undervalued, and undeniably essential funky soul gift. It's a shame the album has yet to be rereleased while so many far more esoteric, lesser LPs have come and gone. It's a fine slice of straight-up, funkyfooted instrumentals, sure-handed and muscular, thanks in large part to Ike's monumental Kings of Rhythm. Here's one of the great bandleaders directing a dynamite collection of musicians, and during the creation of *ABMS*, they were all clearly Feeling It. If there's another forty minutes of this material languishing in a vault, please, somebody, don't keep the world waiting.

The year is 1969, pre-cocaine-era Ike Turner—the version who didn't even like smokin' pot much. (Thinking back to the early 1970s, Ike says he couldn't "handle it"; marijuana made him "unconscious.") Ike and Tina Turner's last worldwide smash, "River Deep, Mountain High," was Back There three years ago in '66, a veritable lifetime when it comes to life on the pop charts. Fortunately the touring revue was still playing shows throughout the world and they remained popular stateside. Before the drugs kicked in hard, before the creative edge got soft, Ike continued working his legendary skinny ass off to maintain what was already a storied career. The hits may not have been forthcoming, but the soulskills themselves were just peaking.

This album plays like Ike's formidable musical resume. There's two playful 1950s R&B tracks (Rufus Thomas's "Philly Dog" and Oliver Sain's "Blacks' Alley") that harken back to the genre he helped nurture early in his career. Two gospel-inspired strolls ("Getting Nasty" and the ecstatic "Freedom Sound") recall childhood musical roots. The album's opening cuts feature fuzz-synthesizer bass lines that sound tastefully outrageous and fresh, but never get to be *too much*. (It's worth noting this particular synthbass sound is very funky-fresh for 1969.)

There's also a late-night juke-joint weeper that steers clear of becoming maudlin ("Nuttin' Up"), with a performance so exuberant yet gentle that only a top-notch band can pull it off with such ease. It's the perfect preamble to the album's final cut, the mini-masterpiece "Freedom Sound." Gushing church organ, long-fingered piano caresses, and punctuations of voices and horns lift the songspirit to God. These songs illuminate the One that defines Black music at its root level. Ike could not have chosen a greater title to represent his finest work, for this album is the very definition of soul music.

When asked about the creation of *A Black Man's Soul*, Mr. Turner couldn't recall many details about the sessions. (Hardly a surprise, as it was recorded more than thirty years ago, and he's come a long way since then.) Ike told me, "All I remember is that I went into the studio and I had no idea what I was going to record. And that's what came out." Apparently the formula worked its magic three decades later with *Here and Now*. "That's the same way I recorded my new album," Ike wrote. So while *A Black Man's Soul* may not necessarily be a full-on planned-out "concept" album, it certainly feels that way. The title itself is a testament to the man and his crack band, with the grooves serving as evidence.

This mighty edition of Ike's Kings of Rhythm really know how to handle the material. They even have the panache to elevate a blatant "Tutti Frutti" rip ("Philly Dog") from being a mere studio toss-off. In lesser hands, this song could have easily turned out sounding like a tired, let's-get-outta-this-damn-studio slice of space filler. But instead, the Ks of R use their confident swagger and infectious energy to great advantage and lend it a solid, necessary bop.

And I'm just talking about what is a decidedly lesser cut on this strong album. Song for song, *ABMS* ranks high with the great classic instrumental R&B/soul albums ever, yet it remains unknown to many beat-heads and funk fans. Ike himself fails to mention its creation and release in his 1999 autobiography, *Takin' Back My Name*. (Hell, even the "detailed" discography in the book's appendix neglects to divulge the album's title!) Upon first listen, you may mistakenly dismiss it as simply being a great party album. However, repeated listenings will reveal a deep, moving, and potent collection of songs that continue to stand the test of time.

A Black Man's Soul, for the uninitiated, contains not just one killer beat but *two*: the beat-head classiques "Funky Mule" and "Up Hard." Just like there's something magical about a clean, shiny vintage 45 leading off with a juicy break, there's a quality equally gratifying when a 12-inch album side introduces itself with a deep drums-only 33⅓ beat. "Funky Mule" does just that when you lay the diamond down on side 2; you're greeted with a 16-count gift to hip-hop, a DJ's dream. There's a pantheon for Phat Shit like this, and never forget it's the great Ike Turner who's givin' it to ya out of his self-theorized (w)hole. (See page 97 of his autobiography for the full scoop on his "hole" theory: every motive and aspect of our lives revolve around holes—no pun intended.)

The album also gives the people another significant break: "Up Hard" (written by Art Miller) is the more relaxed cousin to "Funky Mule." The rhythm of "Up Hard" suggests Allen Toussaint's pulse walking through downtown Memphis, as the pianist frigs the 88s with a firm but playful N'Awlins touch. Inside the song lies an additional fine snatch, with tastyfresh bass drum/snare/hi-hat interplay. It's the very definition of the Old School, and no self-respecting DJ can ever possess enough of 'em.

The Kings of Rhythm have been Ike's band since 1951. The sustained level of high talent throughout its personnel changes is in part a reflection of Ike's ability to surround himself with excellent players, and this cusp-of-the-'70s edition ranks among the tightest and funkiest ever. Bassist Warren Dawson and trapsman Soko Richardson are a righteous rhythm section, their handiwork now a part of hip-hop's foundation. Laying down Strat is firm-fingered Jackie Clark; his guitar darts in and out of the spaces with a wonderfully slinky touch. The savory piano work of Larry Reed is also a must-mention: he even throws in some struttin' Rhodes on two cuts. Coupled with one helluva horn section, and Ike's particular special spices on guitar, piano, and organ, and you've got the ingredients for greatness.

Their combined work on nearly every single song is nothing short of prime—there's very little fat. The performances don't feel overpracticed; in fact, it's as though they're captured right at that first moment of *got-it*. Recorded at a time when soul music was still a strictly singles-driven business and not about producing great full-length LPs, *A Black Man's Soul* stands proud and self-assured, a definite highlight in a what is unquestionably one of American music's most historic oeuvres. ⬤

Wax Poetics *editorial counceleor* J. P. Jones *also makes music, collects records, drinks t'lj beer, and is the editorial production supervisor for a major book publisher.*

Sources:
Author's communiqué with Ike Turner, March 8, 2002.
Ike Turner, *Takin' Back My Name* (Virgin Books, 1999).

Check Your Bucket!
a review of the previously released
by Todd Shanker

Like the strange light and hot tide in the air before a tornado strikes, in the mid-'60s, the broadminded conception of music as a form of creative community communication started illuminating, and circulating within, dilapidated city neighborhoods. This inventive idealism only intensified after the riots in Watts in 1965 and Detroit in 1967. Organizations like Chicago's Association for the Advancement of Creative Musicians (AACM) and Detroit's Tribe, are two of the best examples of how artists and musicians can create sounds that speed like a spiritual ambulance into the dark and almost imperceptible interiors of a community's mindset, and in doing so, at least contribute to a revival of hope.

Both the AACM and Tribe operated on the empirically confirmed logic that a refined sensitivity of communication leads to a more deeply felt understanding and self-knowledge. No doubt, hip-hop's unifying resonance within its blood oath-close crews of MCs, DJs, heads, graffiti artists, and b-boys owes a debt to the AACM/Tribe principles regarding the substance and method of culturally aware rapport.

Emerging from Chicago's Experimental Band, Muhal Richard Abrams (piano) and Roscoe Mitchell (alto, tenor, baritone, bass, soprano, and sopranino saxophones) formed the AACM in May 1965 as an artists' cooperative. Their motto: Ancient to the future. Engrained, but not fossilized, with the grand texture of jazz's evolution from the blues, and the blues' roots in Africa, AACM musicians explored what Amiri Baraka calls the "spiritual past" with a progressive intensity. The result: Adventurous new strategies of improvisation.

Philip Cohran was one of the earliest members of the AACM, and brought to the table an expansive breadth of experience that ranged from searing work on early jump records with Jay McShann to more exploratory improvisation with Sun Ra's Astro-Infinity Orchestra from 1958–1961. In 1967, he released a landmark record on his own Zulu imprint called *On the Beach*. Utilizing a Sun Ra-esque collection of fifteen musicians, Cohran attempted to condense mythopoeic and Afro-centric history into a free, funky, mystical reconnaissance that broke it down like this: Soul is not about superficial symbols or self-righteousness. Like faith, soul is inside you, you just have to search for it and unify with it. Musically, this is a unique record if only for the mesmerizing matrices of fresh sounds and beats. In addition to cornet, Cohran plays a violin uke and a tweaked, amplified West African mbira (thumb piano) that he calls a frankiphone. These idiosyncratic, incandescent sounds—along with Chinese musette, baritone and alto saxophones, trumpet, tuba, trombone, flute, and oboe—map a vast, three-dimensional sphere over a fathoms-deep groove comprised of congas, timbales, trap drums, and stand-up bass.

Several years later, members of the Ensemble—Charles Handy, Don Myrick, Louis Satterfield, and Aaron Dodd—brought their special spiritual geometry to the Pharaohs, a Chi-town collective that formed just blocks north of the 64th Street beach house where Cohran orchestrated the *On the Beach* sessions. The Pharoahs's seminal *Awakening* LP (1971) dropped a rousing celestial funk, a sound and attitude that many of the members would carry with them into the early configurations of Earth, Wind & Fire.

Cohran split-off creatively from the AACM prior to the 1969 birth of the organization's most well-known offspring, the Art Ensemble of Chicago. Formed by Roscoe Mitchell, Lester Bowie (trumpet, flugelhorn, cornet, bugle, pocket trumpet), Malachi Favors (bass), and Joseph Jarman (multiple reeds), this collective created music that connected dead-on with an exciting Afro-ethnic theatricality. This was true performance art, complete with face paint, costumes, stage drama, epic and bold compositions, and all sorts of exotic instrumental combinations, often utilizing Don Moye's virtual village of percussion—hand drums, shekeres, bells, triangles, gongs, claves, tambourines, and many other uniquely crafted rhythm instruments. The Ensemble mined jazz's roots in New Orleans; in early tent

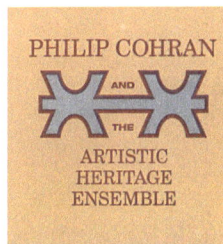

Philip Cohran and the Artistic Heritage Ensemble
On the Beach [reissue title]
(Zulu 1967, Aestuarium 2001)

The Art Ensemble of Chicago
Fanfare for the Warriors
(Atlantic 1973, 4 Men With Beards 2001)

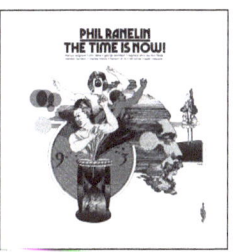

Phil Ranelin
The Time Is Now!
(Tribe 1974, Hefty 2001)

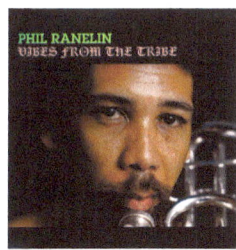

Phil Ranelin
Vibes from the Tribe
(Tribe 1976, Hefty 2001)

shows, churches, bawdy houses, and theater and dance bands; from ragtime to stride to brass band music to bop to modal extrapolations to free jazz and on through its development into a contemporary musical language.

Fanfare for the Warriors is one of the groups greatest records, recorded in 1973, after it returned from the bracingly productive eighteen-month sojourn in Paris that resulted in the equally outstanding *Les Stances a Sophie* (1969), *Message to Our Folks* (1970), and *People in Sorrow* (1969)—not to mention nine other albums! *Fanfare* distinguishes itself from these records with a cliché-free set of compositions so surreal and ceremonial, outlandish and organic, that it forces you to reach out and hold on in the same way a blind man grabs the shoulder of someone he trusts not to lead him over any open manholes. It's music that requires faith in something. Songs like the title cut, "Illistrum," and "The Key" reveal a positivity, a consciousness flush with the instant, the past, and the future. Muhal Richard Abrams' guest spots on piano add depth and dimensionality to an album that successfully evokes the blues of great distances after sunrise as well as the blues of Black expression.

Up in Detroit, the Tribe attempted to heal the deep-rooted scars of the '67 riots with community solidarity and music with a palpable sense of mission. And though comparable to the AACM, the Tribe was undeniably *sui generis* when it formed in 1972. Together, Tribe members such as Phil Ranelin (trombone), Wendell Harrison (tenor sax, flute), Harold McKinney (piano, keyboards), and Marcus Belgrave (trumpet, flugelhorn) were catalytic, churning out surging sounds that aimed to come as close as possible to being an extension of the human soul's vibration. The interesting twist in the Tribe vibe was that almost all the members had served time as session musicians with Motown Records, grooving with Marvin Gaye, the Temptations, and Stevie Wonder, among others. With this vast breadth of experience, and with gigs at Detroit hot and not-so-hot spots like Lowman's Lounge, Showcase, the Strata Gallery, even Alvin's Delicatessen, the Tribe not only sharpened their craft but also connected with the community in an intimate, thoughtful fashion.

The essential characteristic of any tribe is unity. And this Tribe was all about unity of family, race, neighborhood, and humanity. On Phil Ranelin's *Vibes from the Tribe* (1976) and *The Time Is Now!* (1974), his group minted a precise notation of feeling that went way beyond the bugle-blast Black-power propaganda still chic at the time. The subsuming, concentric, often danceable grooves are instantly distinguishable from the more abstract sounds of the Art Ensemble of Chicago. The soulful plunge of Ranelin's trombone and the groove-action of these great Tribe releases from the time has even translated into a recent Hefty project called *The Phil Ranelin Remixes*, with beat-sculptors like El P, Prefuse 73, Nobody, Slicker, and Kirk Degiorgio remixing the Tribe catalogue into the futuristic soundscapes of jungle, downtempo, electronica, and heavy dub, and in the process drawing a connection between free-soul jazz and rave/club/warehouse culture.

The unifying power of the Tribe's music among the Black community became legend. Mayor Coleman Young gave them a key to the city after an especially brisk 1974 concert with guest Donald Byrd on trumpet. The Tribe even performed as the United States representative at the 1976 World Music Festival in Lagos, Nigeria.

The sinuously questing brass and woodwind solos on both *Vibes* and *Time* bring the noise with a congregational quality similar to that of the music-rich services at the Saint John Coltrane African Orthodox Church in San Francisco. Meditative tranquility, spacey exploration, intuitive improvisation, soulful communication, and gelignite-packed sonic fists mingle, react, and then precipitate endothermic and exothermic reactions of ominous intensity. *Time*'s haunting tribute to Trane—"He the One We All Knew"—issues an electric conductivity via ghostly, uncoiling tendrils of spirituality. It's a piece that really emphasizes just how visceral ethereal music can be.

Needless to say these records do not fake the funk. But Tribe was about much more than just music. Tribe was the title of the members' community group, monthly magazine, and record label. The Tribe reached residents with both the immense and the infinitesimal—through crackling local shows, radio programs, word of mouth, and person-to-person, hand-to-hand contact. The Tribe helped residents train for and find jobs, funded a hot breakfast program for children, and offered editorial space to those that wanted to express their opinions and make themselves heard. By successfully bridging the space that separates individuals living side-by-side, the Tribe helped restore a community and the artist's role within it.

It may well be that to understand is to forgive. Art without compassion is very often art in need of passion. This is the reason spiritual, improvised, culture-steeped jazz and soul music like that found on these four records is being reissued with such enthusiasm. Like all classic recordings, these albums are defined not by their dustiness, but their timelessness in both sound and message. ●

Todd Shanker *is a co-author of* MusicHound World *(Visible Ink Press 2000) and just concluded a six-year run writing "House of Stylus," a column covering the best of new and vintage vinyl-available music, for Chicago's* IE *magazine. By day, he is a public defender with the distinction of litigating in both the Illinois and United States Supreme Courts. His more dubious achievements include avoiding judge-hurled gavels with stunning James Brown-like moves, and having his work appear in* Option, Pulse!, The Beat, Alternative Press, *and many other publications.*

Obit: Harold McKinney, composer and pianist, died June 20, 2001, in Detroit, Michigan. He was seventy-two years old.

HIP-HOP ELEMENTS
NEW RELEASES ON EMPIRE MUSICWERKS

GRAVEDIGGAZ
The late Poetic's last heartfelt testament caps the final chapter of the underground hip-hop heroes saga. Featuring Frukwan with guests Prodigal Sunn and Killarmy.

BLUEFACE
The lead force behind Ram Squad Blueface busts out on his own for his full-length debut which will go straight to the heart of hard core hip-hop fans everywhere. Featuring Nelly and Sticky Fingaz.

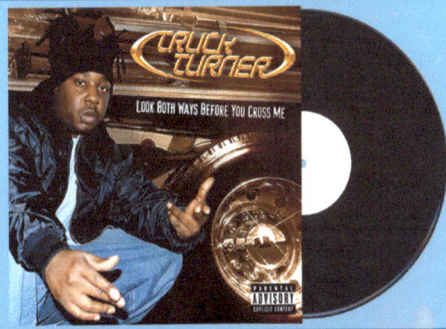

TRUCK TURNER
The long awaited full-length debut from NYC's best kept secret. Truck's supreme metaphoric skills and style flipping is sure to turn a few heads. Truck's gonna run everybody over!

ADEJA BENZ
19 year old hip-hop diva with the attitude and maturity of Teena Marie and the soul of Mary J. Blige. Produced by the inimitable Father MC, one of the originators of the "Uptown" sound and owner of some of the best ears in the business.

Be on the look out for: New albums by Father MC, Wolfpack, Calhouns, 40 Glocc and the solo debut of Frukwan from Gravediggaz

www.empiremusicwerks.com

FIRE CORNER SOUNDS

POOR PEOPLE MUSIC: REBEL ROCK AND THE PRODUCTIONS OF CLIVE CHIN   by Wilson F. Karaman

To label Randy's Studio 17 a mere component of Jamaica's musical evolution would be a misstatement. For the better part of a decade, Randy's *was* Jamaica's musical evolution. In a time of social unrest and global political instability, the modest studio constructed by Vincent Chin at 17 North Parade in Kingston served as a major catalyst in redefining the sound of reggae music. In particular, the early- and mid-1970s productions of Clive Chin, Vincent's eldest son, harnessed the rebellious atmosphere of the day, and in doing so ushered in a new era of progressive music on the Island. By bringing gritty instrumentals and socially conscious lyrics to the people, Clive seized control over a musical revolt that transformed reggae into the predominant median for sociopolitical protest.

The story of Randy's begins in 1959, when Vincent Chin first opened a retail shop on East Street in Kingston. Capitalizing on a newly developing indigenous music industry, Vincent sold independently produced Jamaican records to an increasingly interested public. By 1962, his operation had outgrown its storefront, and the business was moved to its ultimate home over on North Parade. Jamaican autonomy, achieved in August of that year, prompted a further substantial growth in the record industry as people lined the dancehalls in celebration of their new liberation, and Vincent sought to profit by venturing into the realm of production. At the time, recording studios were few and far between, with only a handful of studios renting recording time to freelance producers. For several years, Vincent did his recording at the legendary Federal Studio, scoring with vocal hits by the likes of Lord Creator, Toots and the Maytals, and Alton Ellis. By mid-decade, however, increasing fees and lack of available studio time led to a shortage of recording opportunities for many producers, Vincent Chin included. By 1965, Vincent set in motion a remodeling agenda for his storefront, which included plans to construct a studio above the retail area, and by the fall of 1967, the studio's new foundations had been laid.

With regard to the original recording equipment, Vincent employed Bill Garnett, one of the engineers at WIRL studios, to construct a custom board and console. The initial set up involved a quarter-inch, 2-track Ampex recorder, and was operated by Garnett himself. Since recording time was at such a premium in Kingston, however, Vincent's plan to use Randy's strictly for his own productions quickly proved unfeasible, and the studio was subsequently rented out to other producers. Meanwhile, in order to keep costs down, Vincent involved the help of his family members in running the studio, including Clive. Still a schoolboy at the time, Clive would head to the studio most days after school to help out according to his father's wishes. It was through this rather forced apprenticeship of sorts that Clive would develop and hone his studio skills, which, a couple years down the road, would help mold a new era of Jamaican music.

A turning point occurred for the studio in early 1970, when the chief engineering post changed hands. One of Clive's older schoolmates, a man by the name of Errol Thompson, had been working as an apprentice under engineer Sylvan Morris at the famed Studio One on Brentford Road. After a recommendation from a friend of Vincent's, Errol was offered the job at Randy's. Upon his arrival, he reconstructed the board to suit his taste, and the studio upgraded to a half-inch, 4-track recorder, which allowed for more versatility in the recording process. With Thompson at the controls of a new board, and the young Clive increasingly active in the production process, one of the most important associations in reggae was quickly taking shape.

Reggae music of the late 1960s had become increasingly popularized, as a substantial rift developed within the Jamaican record-listening audience. Sound systems still ruled the urban dancehalls, with DJs providing a live running commentary on metropolitan plight, but it was the more rural, wealthier areas of the Island that accounted for the majority of record sales. Thus, the mainstream hits of the day took on an increasingly soft, even pop-like feel; organ hooks frequently set the melody, and an emphasis on clean production emerged. In fact, period productions by the likes of Lee Perry and Rupie Edwards, while commercially successful, were notable for their rather explicit lack of real political commentary. By the early 1970s, however, this stylistic monopoly would come crashing down.

The end of the 1960s gave way to increasing unrest amongst Jamaica's urban dwellers for several reasons. Political tensions were already running high with the escalation of the war in Vietnam, and a universal unease continued to grip the world as the two nuclear powers of the day, the United States and the Soviet Union, fought proxy battles across the globe. This uneasiness translated very directly to a Jamaican people who had, in nearly ten years of independence from Great Britain, still not reaped the promised fruits of freedom. The nation remained quite poor, and infighting amongst the ruling conservative party, known as the Jamaican Labor Party, resulted in very little reform or economic stimulus. Meanwhile, intensifying protests in America about the country's involvement in Vietnam sparked similar discontent with regard to domestic policy in Jamaica. The minority People's National Party took an increasingly hard-line leftist stance, openly attacking the perceived complacency of then-Prime Minister Hugh Shearer and blaming the conservatives for the country's economic woes. The result was a progressively hostile political climate leading up to the 1972 Parliamentary elections, and an underlying tide of rebellion in the streets. "It was a time of pure revolution," as Clive Chin recalls. "The people was in need of change, and this is when I begin producing. The people need a new way of expressing themself. They need a music for calling attention, a boom-shack-a-lack music."

While the content of Randy's productions did indeed expand farther into the political sphere in the early 1970s, the pace of the music nonetheless preserved its popularized uptempo feel. The Lee Perry-produced *Soul Rebels* album by Bob Marley and the Wailers brought tremendous exposure to the production capabilities of the studio, and while important in introducing the record-buying public to a new lyrical ambition, it still retained a similarly commercial instrumental backing. Furthermore, because the studio was contracted to outside producers a vast majority of the time, commercial potential was a prerequisite for any song released on the studio's house labels (usually Impact!). As Clive recalls, "Impact! was the hit label. My stepmom had the last say on rating the tunes, so she pick the songs that will sell. She not concerned with politics, because politics wouldn't sell!" In fact, until Clive finally ventured into the production arena on his own in late 1971, the vast majority of politically based songs failed to pass auditions at Randy's.

Around this time, the house band at Randy's, known as the Impact Allstars, featured a relatively stable lineup of renowned musicians. The typical lineup included Aston "Family Man" Barrett and Lloyd Adams anchoring the rhythm section on bass and drums respectively, along with Alvin "Reggie" Lewis on rhythm guitar and "Bongo" Ossie Hibbert playing organ, and either Earl "Chinna" Smith or Ronnie Williams rounding out the arrangement on lead guitar. In early 1972, however, Clive brought one of his school friends, a young Horace Swaby, over to the studio during off-hours to record a melody penned by one of his classmates, Dennis Wright. Although he had already scored a hit with his haunting melodica on "East of the River Nile," Swaby, who recorded under the name Augustus Pablo, remained a relatively minor player amongst the Island's musical ranks. This standing, however, would be short-lived following the release of what would become one of the most groundbreaking tracks ever produced during the reggae era. With the Allstars providing a killer rhythmic backdrop, Pablo tore his way through a jolting, highly improvised melodic line.

The completed track, titled "Java," signaled the beginning of a new chapter in Jamaica's musical history book. The slowed tempo of the rhythm section, coupled with Errol Thompson's raw, understated mix, resulted in a vastly different sound to any the public had been accustomed. It was the first song to employ the "rebel rock" sound, and it set a new course for the vast majority of productions to follow for the rest of the decade. "That tune just blow up," Clive remembers. "Yeah, 'Java' was a big tune for me because it was something new. This was poor people music, and it capture the rebel feeling that most people have then. It's a very down-to-earth sound, and the city people, them could relate to it." By this time, the studio

Staged press photo for *This Is...Augustus Pablo*, with Clive Chin posing behind Pablo playing melodica. The Wailers, who played on the album, could not appear in the press photo due to a contract with Island Records.

Mixing down an Augustus Pablo session in 1973. L-R: Dennis Thompson, an assistant engineer; Errol Thompson (on phone), the head Randy's engineer; Clive Chin (in background); and Augustus Pablo.

had upgraded the recording equipment again to one-inch, 8-track, which allowed Clive and Errol Thompson a much more defined sound. By recording the bass directly through a microphone and getting Pablo's melodica on a separate track, Thompson was able to create a very eerie mood for the tune. Clive originally released "Java" on his own side label, Checker, but the immediate demand was so great that the cut was quickly pressed up on Impact! and distributed in mass quantity.

With the upcoming elections of 1972 providing an ample backdrop, the focus of popular music on the Island began to change, and change rapidly. The success of the new instrumental sound developed by Clive, as well as the relative acceptance by the public of politically oriented songs created an environment ripe for a combination of the two. Artists on both sides of the political fence flocked to Randy's to voice their opinions, often resulting in rather scathing personal attacks and indictments. Among others notable for political substance, the Junior Byles-voiced "King of Babylon," produced by Lee Perry, thinly veiled its likening of Prime Minister Shearer to an evil king presiding over a corrupt land. Yet despite the building political interest, Randy's productions other than Clive's remained relatively tame. "My stepmom not into political songs, or the Rasta tunes at all. She pass up [Fred Locks's] 'Black Star Liner'! So I haffi press the more political tunes myself, on my own labels." Over the next couple years he would produce many crucial hits in this vein, employing the vocal talents of such well-respected performers as Dennis Brown, the Heptones, and Freddie McKay, in addition to lesser-known artists like Senya, Ta Teacher Love, and even Ducky Simpson's first incarnation of Black Uhuru.

The Randy's sound, through Clive's productions, developed into a veritable blueprint for conveying messages of social unrest and the hardships of poverty. Defiant vocal cuts like Senya's "Children of the Ghetto," Sweeny's "Won't Come Easy," and Hortense Ellis's cover of "Woman of the Ghetto" tackled tough social issues that had, by and large, previously been ignored in mainstream music. While softer "country reggae" sounds were indeed still receiving attention for their market value in terms of rural music fans, an alternate economy now existed within the production industry in the form of rebel rock. Clive released scores of productions on a plethora of labels, including One Way Sounds, Checker, Giant, Demon, Hot Shot, and Tan-Ya (named after his little sister). In addition to producing vocal cuts, Clive continued to work with a small core of musicians to polish his sound, and Errol Thompson, drawing from the rhythms laid down by these musicians, put together one of the very first dub albums, the elusive *Java Java Java Java* (aka *Java Java Dub*).

Randy's maintained its dominance as the premier studio in Kingston through mid-decade, which provided in-house recordings an immediate spot in the public eye. Clive took full advantage of this situation by reeling off a string of raw hits, including Dennis Brown's seminal "Foot of the Mountain," a Heptones's version of "Guiding Star" (accompanied by a scorching Pablo instrumental), and a remarkable Alton Ellis cover of the Cornelius Brothers's "Too Late to Turn Back Now," where Clive had his musicians build a new rhythm independent of the fast-paced original melody. The result was a bouncy back-and-forth beat with a surprising underlying edge, due in part to Clive's instrumental arrangement, which lacked a rhythm guitar—he instead employed a cheese grater to match Pablo's keyboard on the upbeat.

Meanwhile, Clive had also succeeded in bringing instrumental sounds back to the forefront of the industry. Following his success with "Java," Clive recorded one of the more notable full-length records in Augustus Pablo's *This Is…Augustus Pablo*, which essentially consisted of a collection of cuts featuring Pablo blowing his melodica over the more popular studio rhythms. Several other instrumentals, including a Hortense Ellis b-side version, "Guns in the Ghetto," and Tommy McCook's saxophone run on the "Java" rhythm, titled "Jaro," as well as the Impact Allstars treatment of the popular "Mission: Impossible" theme, also gained attention from the public.

By mid-decade, several new studios became operational in the Kingston area, including the brand new Channel One (constructed by the Hookim brothers), Joe Gibbs Studio, and Lee Perry's musical shrine, the Black Ark.

Although it remained technically open until 1979, Randy's began to lose steam in 1977, when several members of the Chin family relocated to New York (including Clive). Clive would return occasionally over the next two years, presiding over Senya's "Rootsman" session in 1978, and several 1979 Rico sides originally intended for the *Man From Warieka* album. These titles rounded out the Randy's catalog, and the studio officially closed its doors in 1979, perhaps prematurely yet undeniably legendary.

Protest and social strife were the underlying cornerstones of urban life for Jamaicans of the early 1970s, and thanks to the vision of Clive Chin the people gained a primary outlet for expression through music. This outlet was made possible first and foremost by the success of Randy's in essentially cornering production in Kingston. As Earl Morgan of the Heptones recalls, "Everybody record at Randy's. If yuh nah record deh, nobody know you." With the majority of the industry's attention and resources concentrated on Randy's, Clive assumed a very powerful position at the dawn of his producing career, and indeed used this position to his advantage very effectively. He combined conscious lyrics with deep, brooding melodies to create a brand new sound. In doing so, Clive introduced the general public to the potential power of music as a social force, and thus effectively carved out a new path for the industry, one that would be followed by countless subsequent producers throughout the 1970s. The rebel rock sound was a raw and determined voice, and it belonged to the poor.

Wilson Karaman is a freelance writer and student in New York City. He can be heard every Monday night at 8:00 spinning roots reggae and dub as host of the "Fire Corner Sound System" radio program on WNYU 89.1 FM. You can also track him down at Jammyland Records, located at 60 East 3rd Street (between 1st and 2nd Avenues) in Manhattan.

Sources:
Steve Barrow, liner notes from *Forward the Bass: Dub From Randy's, 1972–1975* (Blood and Fire Records, BAFCD 022, 1998).
Author's interview with Clive Chin, New York City, January 19, 2002.
Author's interview with Earl Morgan, New York City, December 13, 2001.

RECOMMENDED LISTENING:

Augustus Pablo *This Is…Augustus Pablo* (Above Rock Records)

The current pressing of this record, re-released in 1997, includes all twelve original cuts (the CD version has two bonus tracks, including the elusive "Java Original.") One of the premier all-instrumental albums ever recorded, this collection provides a dozen examples of the early rebel rock sound—a must.

Impact Allstars *Forward the Bass: Dub From Randy's, 1972–1975* (Blood and Fire)

This is a solid collection of early dub shots to come out of Randy's, mixed mainly by Errol Thompson at the height of Clive's popularity as a producer. Several *Java* cuts, as well as a few lesser-known rhythms. This album is a stellar example of early dubbing techniques—while King Tubby's studio had the luxury of sliding faders, making it possible to ease tracks in and out of the mix, Randy's still relied on pushing buttons. While the result may seem like a more rudimentary mix, Thompson's innovations of adding sound effects and a constant delay created a stylistically unique sound.

Impact Allstars *Java Java Java Java* (Impact!)

If you can find it, this is one of the most historically important albums to own. Unfortunately, it remains without a widely available re-pressing (a fact that will hopefully change soon), and as a result it has become all the more widely sought after by collectors. Ten largely drum-and-bass versions of top Randy's rhythms in their most raw form. Happy hunting…

Various Artists *17 North Parade: Clive Chin Productions* (Pressure Sounds)

London-based Pressure Sounds provided a great service to the record-buying public with this collection. These are the essentials, conveniently collected on one piece of wax for your listening pleasure. The CD does contain more tracks than the vinyl, but you won't be disappointed with either. Contains most of Clive's early vocal hits, as well as several less well-known tracks and a couple rare instrumentals.

The Memoirs of **Prince Paul**

as told to Andrew Mason

I'VE BEEN COLLECTING

RECORDS FROM THE TIME I WAS FIVE YEARS OLD. A LOT OF GUYS PROBABLY SAY THAT, BUT I STILL HAVE SOME OF THE RECORDS I GOT BACK THEN. I BOUGHT "GROOVE ME" [BY KING FLOYD] WHEN IT CAME OUT, "HOT PANTS" [BY JAMES BROWN] WHEN IT CAME OUT…*SPIDER MAN*, THE ONE ON BUDDHA RECORDS THAT HAD A ROCK BAND ON IT. EVERYBODY IN MY HOUSE BOUGHT RECORDS SO IT JUST SEEMED LIKE THE THING TO DO. IN HINDSIGHT, I GUESS IT WAS A LITTLE STRANGE FOR A FIVE-YEAR-OLD KID TO BUG HIS FOLKS OVER A RECORD. I WANTED TOYS TOO, BUT I WOULD CRY OVER A RECORD. I HAD A MICKEY MOUSE TURNTABLE, WHERE YOU PUT HIS ARM DOWN ON THE RECORD TO PLAY IT. MY MOM TOLD ME THAT EVEN WHEN I WAS A BABY, I WOULD CRY WHENEVER THE MUSIC BOX IN MY CRIB WOULD RUN OUT; SHE HAD TO KEEP WINDING IT UP.

I'm the youngest in my family. When I came along my brothers and sister were teenagers, and I was familiar with whatever they were playing around the house. My father was a hardcore jazz fan, like Thelonious Monk, not easy listening stuff. My mom was really into true soul music: Al Green, Marvin Gaye, Syl Johnson.

The first time I heard anything remotely hip-hop, I was ten years old. Back then I was shuttling between Amityville, Long Island, and Brooklyn, where my grandmother lived. I remember hearing about Herc, Bambaataa, DJ Flowers, and around '78, I heard of Flash. That's when I started to trying to DJ. Flash was always the guy. Back then everybody played the break off Karen Young's "Hot Shot," Cameo's "Serious." I'm talking about just throwing in stabs, not scratching at all. Then when scratching came in, that's when I first started hearing about [Grand Wizard] Theodore, and him battling Flash.

I would go to jams in the parks and everybody would be dancing, but my whole focus would be on the DJ. Not that they were doing tricks or anything, but, oh my God, just the records they played. That was when they used to cover up the labels on everything. But the DJs weren't that bright because back in the crates they would have the sleeve sticking up. I would be looking behind them saying, "I *have* that record!" Pleasure, "Joyous"—had that. "Down on the Avenue," Fat Larry's Band—had that. Dexter Wansel, "Life on Mars"—had that, or my brother had it. Whatever he had I considered it mine! [*laughs*] I had a lot of those same records in the house somewhere, and watching those DJs inspired me.

When I got into the sixth grade I put a crew together with my friends that lived across the street, the Eveready Crew. They told me, "We're going to start a crew, and you're going to be the DJ." That's when all the teasing began. Think about it, this little kid in sixth grade trying to be a DJ. Everybody called me "Fake Grandmaster Flash"!

Initially, DJing was just for the love of the music, and to get recognized. I wasn't a jock, I didn't play sports, I wasn't super smart, didn't have all the girls. DJing was a way to make people notice me. For a guy who had been nobody, faded into the cracks in the wall, it made me stand out.

Time passed and I progressed as a DJ, and by the 9th grade I was considered one of the best in my local circle. At that time I didn't have 1200s, of course; I was using B1s and this big silver Gemini mixer. I gave that to the [Hip-Hop] Hall of Fame people. And what bugged me out was looking at the other stuff they had there: Flash's mixer, DST's mixer—we were all using the same model.

For a while in junior high school I used to spin for Biz Markie; he was my MC. This was in '81 or '82. Back then he was called Bizzy Bee. Yeah, there was another Bizzy Bee but this was the Bizzy Bee of Long Island! He would come over religiously after school and we would make mixtapes and go back and forth, tipping each other off on beats: "You got this? You got *this*?"

We had a whole little scene out there on Long Island. Rakim was coming up, he had a group called the Love Brothers, they used to call him Pop, or the Love Kid Whiz. They used to battle another group called Supreme Force [who later recorded for Nia], which was Freddy C [Freddy Foxx] and Chili Dog, who was down with Groove B Chill. If you went further west out to Hempstead, you had Chuck D and Bill Stephney with the Mr. Bill Radio Show. I remember going out to a high school in Central Islip to battle Diamond J, who later spun for EPMD. Back then Parrish was in a group called the Rock Squad.

I was into all the tricks, under the leg, with the mouth. A lot of people don't know that was my primary thing. I used tricks to beat people and that's how Biz and a lot of other people got down with me. It's called turntablism now but if you hear a lot of my scratches from back then they were ahead of their time. In "Just Say Stet," for example, I was breaking up words [sings the *"fun-ky"* from James Brown's *"Funky President"*], trying to invent stuff. As insane as people think I am on production—you know, thinking up ill stuff—I put that energy into my scratches, like, *No one's ever done* that *before!*

I also thought differently from a lot of people, at least DJing-wise, and that made me stand out. I would play things like Herb Alpert's "Spanish Flea," "Batman's Theme." Awkward songs, weird stuff just to bug people out! That comes from listening to Bambaataa, he was ill like that. What I didn't realize was that he had power and juice so he could play stuff like that and people would listen. Who's going to dis Bam?! He was the man! He ran a big portion of the Bronx, he could play whatever he wanted to! Not with me, I'd throw these records on and people would go, "He's buggin'!" and say I'm being stupid and all. But I had a lot of records that people weren't running, especially out on LI; you just wouldn't hear them. I collected anything and everything and had all this obscure stuff to cut back and forth. I still have beats today that I've never heard anybody use.

I was out on the *Deep Concentration* tour with Peanut Butter Wolf and Cut Chemist, and we went record shopping in Florida. I found so many old school breakbeat records. I'd blatantly put it in front of their faces, and they'd go, "What's that?" I was like, *Perfect! They don't even know what it is!* That was a good gauge. "You don't know this?! Okay." And I'd put it aside, not say anything more. There are a lot of records from that time that got overlooked, only the popular ones are really known about.

When comps like *Ultimate Breaks* came out it was kind of cool, but at the same time it made me mad. For real collectors and DJs it was traumatic. You know, you're there covering up your labels and all that, and those breakbeat records exposed a lot. There would be stuff on there that I had that *nobody* had. *Super Disco Breaks*, the *Octopus* joints—they would come out and I'd be like, *"Ahgh!"* I can't front, I bought them, still have them, but some of the records I had that made it special when I rocked the party were on there and now anybody could go buy it. To me, as far as beat collecting, breakbeat compilations ruined everything. It just took the fun out of it. I'm glad I'm not as emotional and sensitive as I was back then when that was my forte. In those days I was like, *Man, that's wack.* But you just try to stay one ahead, one up. Especially when I started working with De La. It would be like, *Y'all are thinking of using this, well let me show you something you weren't even* thinking *of* using. Something that's right in your face! There's a lot of stuff like that.

SURGEON ON THE MIX

I met Stet at a DJ battle in Brooklyn. I was a total b-boy back then, Kangol like LL had, Lees, green and blue Nikes, and a name belt that said PAUL on it. At that time the group consisted of Daddy-O, Delite, Grand Supreme, and Wise. Daddy-O had these long braids down his back. They wore all white and had some spikes like the Furious Five. When they rolled up on me I thought it was a gang. They were like, "That's him!" Mind you, I'm a teenager, probably sixteen, and they're saying, "You got it! You got it!" I said, "Got what? Hey, I'm not from around here!" They said, "You got what we're looking for!" They had just done the Mr. Magic Rap Attack show and won a contest and they wanted me to be their DJ. Although I was living in LI at the time, I was down. I'd send them tapes of different records, beats and stuff, and we'd meet up on the weekends and rehearse. I had no idea at the time what I was getting into. We were supposed to sign with Sugar Hill, but the contract was bad. We ended up signing with Tommy Boy, where the contract was also bad, but not as bad as the Sugar Hill one. Everybody was worried that I was too young to sign; I think I was seventeen or something.

DBC came in, and he was a keyboard player, he played by ear. Wise would beatbox, and I would scratch over that. When we did "Go Stetsa I" from *On Fire*, we had a drummer friend of Daddy-O's [Nawthar Muhammad] come in and play. Once all the elements were together, we were like, *That's insane!* That was where the idea of the hip-hop

Prince Paul photos by Andrew Mason

band came from. It wasn't until afterwards that we met Bobby [Simmons, aka Fruitkwan]. The first tour we went out with two DJs (they gave DBC a set), and Wise was the human beatbox. That was the LL Cool J tour for Def Jam in 1987, my first tour. When we were embarking on the second album, we thought of getting the live drums officially into our act. We already were known for having a great show. We had a keyboard player, which nobody really had at the time, DJ, and human beatbox—and the drummer just made it complete. That's when we started saying, "We are the hip-hop band." It was first stated on "Go Stetsa," but that was when it became a reality.

Making *On Fire* was my first time in a "real" studio. I didn't know what I was doing back then, and I remember watching Bob Power really closely, actively trying to figure stuff out. He kind of broke my spirits by telling me, "You'll never learn this by watching me." I was like [*hangs his head*], "Oh…Okay." *I'll figure this out on my own.* As far as producing, I really didn't know what it was. All I knew was that I made beats, and I knew what I liked and didn't like. Daddy-O was really running the show at the time. I just put my two cents in.

Everything was innocent at the time. I was going to school, trying to graduate college, and get a regular job. The band was just a hobby, fun stuff, you know? I'd always worked a side gig, even in the midst of making records with Stet and De La. I worked with Nationwide Metric—a metric nut and bolt company—General Accident Insurance Company, a lot of places.

Ironically enough, I had a music appreciation course in college. Everybody there was into rock, Duran Duran,

whatever was popular at the time. I was kind of in my own world. We had to do a project and people were doing things like making a guitar, or doing a report on the origins of rock and roll. Now, in music appreciation, you are supposed to appreciate all music, and hip-hop was not respected *at all*. I announced, "I'm doing rap music," and everybody turned around and just gave me a nasty look. Now mind you, I'm one of maybe two Black kids in the class. The other guy turned to me and whispered "You're blowing it!" [*laughs*] The teacher said, "What, 'rad' music?" I said, "No, R-A-P. Hip-hop." The teacher sighed, and was like, "Okay." I put all this thought and anger into that report and ended up getting an A+. I used illustrations, wrote about the culture, how there's graffiti, dancing, there's the DJ, the MC. I wrote in the first paragraph that "those who are close-minded won't get it," psychologically setting it up so that you wouldn't want to be the close-minded person. I remember I used to get *dissed* though. Rap got no respect.

The guys in Stet were real dismissive of college and told me, "You don't need to do that, we're going to blow up!" I was like, "Man, we ain't blowing up nothing!" 'Cause I had seen the money we made and I knew I had to go to school and get a job. The irony is that I took that approach and I'm still here making records while they had to go and get regular jobs. I don't mean to make it sound funny, but it's just ironic because our philosophies were totally different. I never cared about who was wearing the gear or who was doing what, and that got to be their focus, following trends. *Three Feet High* was a total rebellion against that whole mentality.

THE MENTOR AND HIS THREE SONS

I met Mase through a record my music teacher from high school was trying to put out. His name was Everett Collins and he used to play drums on tour for the Isley Brothers. There was a rapper named Gangster B who had a group called Play Hard, his song was called "Cold Waxin' the Party" [eventually released on Alexadon Records, 1988]. That's the first record with Mase's voice on it. You want to search for a record? Try finding that one! This was when I had first joined Stet and he had me come in and program a beat on the Sequential Tom drum machine. They wanted me to do this backwards beat like how the Beasties did on "Paul Revere." I thought, *Nooooo! I can't do that, that's wack!* I mean, "Paul Revere" is a great song, but to bite, especially in close proximity to when the original record came out, that's not my style. But they persuaded me and so I programmed it. They were loving it, but me and Mase were sitting there like, *Oh, this is wack!* So Mase says to me, "I've got this project called De La Soul, and whatever you want to do, we're down." I'm like [*grins fiendishly*], "Word?"

Mase came by the house later that day with a really rough tape of "Plug Tunin'." They had done the beat collectively. Immediately I thought, *This is really ill, it's just missing a few things*. I dubbed some stuff over it, kind of redid it, and told Mase that I wanted to meet the guys.

When they eventually came over I was like, *You?!* Especially Dave [Trugoy]. I was always a big nerd in school but he was way nerdier than me. Pos—I knew his brother was a thug—so I kinda gave him credit like maybe he was a thug too, but he was just as nerdy! It was so weird, they were the guys you'd least expect to rhyme. I played them what I did and they were all into it. I used Manzel, "Midnight Theme," from the 45. The other thing we used was a record that belonged to Pos's father [the Invitations, "Written on the Wall" (Dynovoice)]. Tommy Boy had a contest to see if anyone could discover what that song was, and nobody ever really came to the table. It was also a 45, and the irony of it was that on the side we used, it said "Plug Side." They were already calling themselves Plug One and Two; I thought they were crazy! They told me, "You know, when you plug in the mic?"—and had me say that in the beginning [of "Plug Tunin'"] to kind of set the concept up.

Everybody pooled their money together and we made the demo at Calliope. I had thought, *Let's just do it right, 24-track and all*. I don't know what made me think that, it was just the blind leading the blind! *Hey, let's waste money!* Who knows, I just wanted to act like I knew what I was talking about; I was only twenty! I'd be in the studio, not really knowing much but having heard stuff in sessions with Stet, and I'd say things like, "Yeah, let's compress that…" not really knowing what I was doing! I had a crazy imagination about how to get stuff done and it just kind of worked out.

So we did the demo, and I gave it to Daddy-O, 'cause he was the guy with the juice back then. I used to look up to him, you know, he was so smart and he knew everybody. He was shopping this guy named Frankie J at the time, a keyboard player. I gave him the demo to take with him, and every place he went was like, "Ehh, Frankie J, but *these* guys…" So all the attention got on them. It was funny though, I brought De La to the studio one time to watch Stet, so they could familiarize themselves with how the process works and all, and Stet were like, "Why'd you bring these guys here?"—really making them feel bad. When I was making their demo I asked Daddy-O if he wanted to get down with me because I really respected him, and he was like, "Nah, they sound too much like Ultramagnetic."

But I had him keep shopping it, and a lot of people liked it. We got offers from Profile, Geffen, and Tommy Boy. I wanted to go with Profile. They offered a lot more money, and they had Run-DMC, plus I had already dealt with Tommy Boy through Stet and I didn't want to go there. Geffen was offering us a big chunk of money for its day, more than twenty thousand. But De La liked [Tommy Boy President] Monica Lynch, so they decided on Tommy Boy.

When "Plug Tunin'" started getting plays, Merce [Pos] and Dave were amazed. I had made them not tell anybody that they had a record coming out until it was released because of the pressure in the neighborhood, people bothering them. I just remember them being happy. They were the most thankful guys back then. That's how I became "The Mentor," "Poppa Prince Paul." I really didn't know much, but I would tell them just about anything to keep their spirits up. You know, like, "Don't worry about it, our first album's gonna go gold," this and that. With Stet, I was the youngest member and I always had difficulty getting my point across. They would say, "Ahh, young boy doesn't know what he's talking about." So I wanted to prove to them, and to myself, that I really did know what I was talking about (even though I didn't!), that I really had a voice. Plus I had been telling De La the whole time that it would work out, and I realized that I really had to make it happen!

SKIP 2 MY LOOPS

As far as beatmaking in De La went, everybody had a ton of ideas about what to use. My role was showing them how to put things together. They had a general idea of what they wanted to do, it could be just a couple records, and I'd take it and completely overproduce it. [*laughs*] That was my whole thing on that album: overproduction! I was like, "Yeah, that's cool, but let's add this," "Man, that snare doesn't really work, add this," et cetera.

Pos would bring in records, Mase would bring in records, Dave would bring in records sometimes. It's like a little competition, and I think that's how that album elevated. *You think this is hot, well check* this *out*—you know? There was a lot of ego involved, us trying to outdo each other, and I would not be outdone! *Watch me put* this *together*. "Yeah, that part's cool, but let's loop this part." That was my role, literally telling them exactly what to do. I used to give them homework assignments at the end of every studio session: "Okay, when we come in tomorrow, you need your sixteen bars for this, bring in this record, I know you got it, Pos. Mase, you're going to need to do scratches on this…" I was a control freak, and still am to some extent. That's probably why we don't work together now, I want things exactly the way I want them.

At the time I started working with De La, sampling had just become popular. But I didn't want to do what everybody was doing at the time, just have a loop of one thing with maybe some scratches on it. I was going to layer my samples, have horns, everything's going to match, everything's going to be in tune. That, in my opinion, is the claim to fame of that record. Not just obscure samples, but how layered everything is. Some of that I bit off the Bomb Squad. I also listened to Dre, with "Eazy-Duz-It." I listened to all of that, and thought, *I'm going to take it to the next level, flip it a little extra.* One, by using different records; two, by layering different stuff that you wouldn't even think about using together. "Say No Go" is a perfect example. There's so much in there: Sly Stone, Hall and Oates, the Emotions, and everything's in tune.

The bulk of the De La records came from battling for beats between me and Pos. A lot of times we'd be in the studio, a loop would be playing and we'd throw stuff on the turntable to see what would work and try to blend it in. It's a DJing thing. "Eye Know," with the Mad Lads and Steely Dan, came out of that.

I am a goofy guy to begin with, and I just brought that out of them in the studio. They would ask me, "Are you sure?" and I'd just encourage it all. Like with the Barry White thing ["I'm Gonna Love You a Little Bit More, Baby"], I always wanted to use that. We were in the studio with Q-Tip, Red Alert, MC Lyte, a whole bunch of people were there that day. I looped it up, and said, "I want to call this one…'De La Orgy'! Everybody go in the booth and just moan!" They were still kids, I was still a kid—we were just being stupid, having fun. I always wanted to do stuff like this, but with Stet it wouldn't have fit. [De La] looked up to me, it was a different role; I opened up a side of them. You know, *Whatever Paul says goes, he made Stetsasonic.* I just lucked out that I had somebody to be my little robots at the time.

They inspired me too, because they made me do things I wouldn't have done either. They were so into, *We will* not *be seen as this, this is corny*—you know, elements in the culture at the time that they weren't having. It gave me that attitude as well, they brought that out of me and it's stuck with me to this day.

I got a weird vibe from the people in Stet after the success of De La. Daddy-O has always been the leader of Stet and I'm cool with that. I don't mind being the DJ in the back. At that point though, when we would do interviews and things people would focus on me and he was no longer the man. I could see the guys in the group get a little upset, and I didn't want that. From that point on things just got really weird. That was in between *In Full Gear* and the last Stet album. We just stopped calling each other and Stet broke up unofficially.

FROM THREE FEET HIGH TO SIX FEET DEEP

After *Three Feet,* I was getting approached to do so much work. I remember immediately Serch approached me, like, "You know how you did 'Buddy,' with other cats rhyming on it? We want to do something like that," and that became "Gas Face." Kane, Latifah, it just went on and on. If I was as popular now as I was then I'd be a millionaire! But rap was so new back then. I was making good money but in comparison to now…it's like Dr. Jay compared to Jordan. You're still ill, but the times and the money are different. It was surreal though. I remember there was this truck I wanted, a Dodge 4×4, and I thought, I'll just do a remix, go straight to the dealer. I wasn't one to splurge money but it was strange to think all of a sudden I could do a remix and buy a car!

I didn't intend to make any more De La Soul records. It was going to be this record and then let them do their own thing. I told them, you're on your own, you know how to work stuff in the studio, but they really wanted me to work with them on the next record. They considered me part of the group, Plug Four. I was flattered and we did the next one.

I remember with *De La is Dead,* just trying to keep everything under wraps. I'm a private guy and I don't like a lot of people knowing what I'm working on, or listening to too much stuff. It was hard due to the popularity of the first album; everyone was curious to see what we were coming with next.

De La got so big so quickly, it was strange. People expected one thing out of them and didn't necessarily get it. The first album was a lot of my personality, and they weren't necessarily like that. They got kicked off the LL Cool J tour for fighting. "Your boys just beat up this person…" Yo, I'd hear that all the time. "Pease Porridge" came out of a real incident. So with the second album you hear a lot more anger. I still wanted to keep the vibe of the first album but I had to respect the fact that they were growing.

With *Buhloone Mindstate,* a lot of times it was just Pos and me in the studio. Mase contributed a lot on that one as well, but separately. That's how that album was constructed, really fragmented. You could tell we were moving apart at that point. The stuff that came out on the *Clear Lake Auditorium* EP for example, they did that on their own. I was there to record the vocals but that was it. When I think about that album, the vibe was almost gloomy. Everybody was doing their own thing.

What really hurt me at the time was when Serch was starting his solo record. He told me he was talking to Russell [Simmons] and told him he wanted me to produce some songs. Russell said, "Paul? Why you want to use him? He's played out. He's out of here." I got sad for a while. A lot of stuff seemed to be going wrong at that time. People were saying my De La stuff wasn't as good anymore, I had put a lot into Dew Doo Man Records and that stuff never came out. People like Pete Rock and Large Professor were coming up and my stuff hadn't been out there in a while. I felt like I was getting dissed and that's when I began to put together the Gravediggaz.

I sat down, depressed, angry at the world, making all these dark songs. I just thought I would put together a whole bunch of undesirables, rebelling against everybody again. First I contacted RZA. I [had] met him at Calliope, doing "Ooh We Love You Rakeem." He had a loop and I programmed a beat under it as a rough idea of what to do, expecting he would change it. The next thing I know the record came out with my beat on it. But at the time he didn't really have a lot going on, he had just gotten out of some trouble with the law. Poetic was homeless. Fruitkwan was making clothes or something. We were all Tommy Boy rejects! The concept of the group was to pool our resources and uplift each other.

We got together at my house. RZA brought Genius and Ol' Dirty with him, who at the time was called A-Son. Everybody just freestyled, got to know each other. This was before Wu-Tang had coalesced. It's funny in hindsight, Wu asked me if I could do some beats for them but I turned it down to focus on the Gravediggaz project. When RZA first played me a tape of his beats I didn't know what to think. It wasn't even as polished as the stuff he's done that became popular. It was some really awkward stuff. Back then he often sat down and asked me questions about producing and mixing. I lent him the record he used for the beat under "Wu-Tang Clan Ain't Nuthing ta F' Wit" [Biz Markie's "Nobody Beats the Biz"]. He tried to keep it too! I had to go over his crib and snatch it back. [*laughs*]

RZA recorded stuff really rough—kind of like how I did in the beginning with De La—not really knowing what he was doing. At that point I was becoming a technical-head, working with sequencers on the computer, trying to get stuff sound a certain way. Watching RZA really brought me back to the raw guts of the music and not the technology behind it. I owe a lot to him for bringing me back to that.

It took a long time to get a deal for Gravediggaz, even though to me that demo was incredible. Everyone was getting discouraged and wanted to quit, but finally we were

signed by Gee Street. By this time RZA had pressed up "Protect Ya Neck" on his own and that was making some noise, so he wasn't as into it as he had been. Gee Street wasn't even going to sign him as part of the group, in fact. It's ironic, because after Wu-Tang blew up, he became the focus of the group.

The second record [*The Pick, the Sickle and the Shovel*] wasn't really supposed to happen. When we got together I made it clear to everyone that this was a one-shot thing. I think what happened though, is that Poetic and Fruitkwan mismanaged their money. RZA took off, and I wasn't feeling like a Gravedigga no more. That was when I began working on *Psychoanalysis*. RZA and I didn't really want to do this new Gravediggaz album, but we felt like we were letting the other two down 'cause that was all they had going on. But RZA had just formed a production team, and I came up with the idea that RZA could hand the production work to his boys, get them work, we don't leave Poetic and Fruitkwan stranded and it would be good all around. So I didn't really do anything at all on that album.

PSYCHOANALYSIS AND BEYOND

Psychoanalysis was a record that nobody was supposed to hear. Skiz [WordSound Records CEO] had talked to me a while back and told me eventually he was going to have this label and when he did would I do an album for him. I agreed, and forgot about it until a few years later he calls me and says, "Remember that label I told you about? I want you to do the record for us." He was only going to press up about 1,000 copies, so I said, "Okay, that's cool, we'll split the profits and that'll be it."

Even though the Gravediggaz had done well commercially, the reviews were pretty critical, calling it a "horror-core fad" and things. I was fed up with the whole music business too, and had been thinking of just moving down south, opening up a Jiffy Lube or Dunkin' Donuts, just getting out entirely. This record [*Psychoanalysis*] was supposed to seal my fate. Everything on it is, I won't say horrible, but it's not meant for people to like. It's me and a bunch of my friends from high school on tracks that nobody ever liked, a lot of really old 4-track and 8-track recordings. The irony of it is that it resurrected my career instead of burying it. People actually liked it. Chris Rock called me, said he had heard it, and asked me to work with him. I couldn't believe it. Then there was a bidding war between Tommy Boy and Gee Street over who was going to pick up *Psychoanalysis*! I was like, *You've got to be kidding!*

I met Automator when he asked me to do a remix for Dr. Octagon's "Blue Flowers." We started talking and had a lot of things in common, we were using a lot of the same drum machines, watched the same TV shows. In fact that's how the name *Handsome Boy Modeling School* came about—from [Chris Elliot's short-lived TV show] *Get a Life*.

My next record is going to be me biting everybody's style. That's the concept. Biting in 2002 is no longer a crime so I'm taking advantage of that. You will hear all those things that you've never heard me do before. It's called *Politics of the Business*. I tried to make it sonically as close to a Jay-Z record as possible. Smoothed it out! I even made beats on there using no samples whatsoever. I wanted to make an album that's EQed right and won't slow the party down, where I can play it out when I'm DJing, and people will hopefully stay on the floor! It may be my best record, but my least favorite 'cause it doesn't embody me as much.

I try to come from the heart when I make beats. I have an understanding of what makes a radio hit, but for me to just copy that style would be a little insincere. There's always a twist to it. I just do what I like and what I feel, I rarely compromise. I think that's real important. When people look back, when they look at my entire body of work, it gives a good description of who I am, and I'm proud of it—my son and his kids' kids can be proud of. To me that's it. I'm not going to bling it out if it's not me and I can't back it up. I do crazy records, fun records, stuff that I think is creative, and fortunately I have a following that appreciates that. I've gone against a lot of people's advice, fired a lot of people; I've always gone against the grain, thinking that every time I make a record it could be my last. But I just do it anyway 'cause I can't make those regular records.

How farfetched is making rap records and staying in business for any length of time? It's so trendy. One day you're hot and the next you're not. I never would've thought I could be in it for this long. I never planned on being a producer. I never planned on making records. I never planned on making music a career. It all evolved from loving music and loving the art. To this day it amazes me that I wake up and make records. How wild is that? ⭕

Andrew Mason, aka DJ Monk-1, is a former short-order cook and welterweight dub champion. His selections can be heard weekly on the "Underground Railroad" radio show (WBAI 99.5 FM) and at the Greenhouse in Brooklyn, NY. He never did find out what "Strictly Dan Stuckie" means.

Prince Paul's All-Time Top Records:

"Flash It to the Beat" (live, Bozo Meko version) Grandmaster Flash

"Rock the Bells" (original version) LL Cool J

"My Melody/Eric B for President" Eric B & Rakim

"My Mic Is on Fire" Lord Shafiyq

"Holy War" Divine Force

It Takes a Nation of Millions to Hold Us Back Public Enemy (my all time favorite rap album)

Licensed to Ill Beastie Boys (any of Rick Rubin's Productions)

Enter the Wu-Tang (36 Chambers) Wu-Tang Clan

Niggaz4Life NWA; *The Chronic* Dr. Dre (any of Dre's Productions)

Innervisions Stevie Wonder

Motor Booty Affair Parliament (my all time favorite record ever)

I'm Still in Love with You Al Green

"Plug Tunin'"

We had a skit on that first single. I was doing little bug-out pieces for [Long Island radio personality] P-Fine, and we took that concept and basically put it on the record. I called them bug-out pieces, and it wasn't until later that the media started calling them skits. We used to hang out at one of our cribs with a Casio SK-1 [sampling keyboard] and just laugh and talk, with the tape recorder on, and that's where that came from. We just thought it was funny and said let's just put it on there.

Dew Doo Man Records/Resident Alien

Dew Doo Man Records came about because Lyor Cohen called me and said [Def Jam] wanted to do a label with me. I wasn't interested, but he was persistent. I talked to my lawyer, he broke it down for me and it seemed like it would be easy enough. I got to put out x number of acts a year, produce them and all. I was thinking, alright, this could be good, I'll put on all my friends from the neighborhood. So I meet up with Russell [Simmons], he wanted to call it Prince Paul Records. I never took it seriously, and told him I wanted to call it Dew Doo Man Records. Russell was like, "Ahh, you don't want to call it that." I insisted on it and Russell reluctantly agreed. I sketched up the idea for the logo and he just shook his head.

So I just signed up all my friends and what happened was after the first record, although the reviews were good, Russell and them weren't feeling it. The whole album [Resident Alien's *It Takes a Nation of Suckers to Let Us In*] was done, but they kept on putting off the release date of the LP. They had just signed EPMD, they had to put out LL's new one, and of course my material was getting older. So as time passed it became obvious that neither side was feeling the label idea so I approached Russell and we just deaded it.

Turtles "You Showed Me" 45

We gave Tommy Boy a list of all the samples to every song on the first album. It was up to them to decide what to clear. They cleared obvious stuff like George Clinton, and I guess they thought the Turtles weren't popular enough to bother with. It just so happens that the daughter of one of the guys from the Turtles was listening to the De La record and he hears something in the other room that sounded familiar. "That's my record!" So he makes the call, and then the big suing thing began. I guess the Turtles weren't popping at the time, *Three Feet High and Rising* was a popular record, and they wanted to get paid. They didn't seem to really see any artistry behind it. All I remember was Tommy Boy asking us a lot of questions about the sample, the loop, this and that. We were like, it's just a bug-out piece, it's not even a real song! I remember it being a big deal, and me not caring. I couldn't care less. Because I'd never made any money from making records anyway, it was just another record to me and I didn't know it would affect my money, my royalties, let alone anything else.

Hardcore

Hardcore was the first record I ever produced. The first thing I did outside of Stet, around the same time as I was hooking up with Stet. Those were kids from around the way. One of the kids in the group made the beats. I took "producer" to mean the person who oversaw it, arranged it and all. The beatmaker was this guy Double B who was later in Resident Alien. We're all kinda close-knit.

Fine Young Cannibals

Fine Young Cannibals was kind of pushed on me. I had gotten down with Rush Management and they would say yes to people without asking me. So they already committed to do it and I felt pressured into it. I was constantly getting into predicaments with them and that's why I eventually left. Why could I do a 3rd Bass record for say $3,000 and then do Fine Young Cannibals for $20,000? Because it was Def Jam. It was a conflict of interest. Rush was setting the price for my work. The final straw was when they owed me for work I had done, and they had gotten paid for it but used it to pay somebody else, telling me they'd pay me later.

I turned down a lot of remix work because I wasn't feeling the songs. Janet Jackson's "Black Cat," for example. The B-52's sent me a tape of "Love Shack" before it came out, they were big fans and wanted to know if I'd remix it. I listened to it and couldn't really think of anything for it; I gave it to Daddy-O to do.

Gear:

DRUM MACHINES/SAMPLERS/SEQUENCERS:
Sequential Circuits Tom
Oberheim DX
Roland TR-808
Roland TR-909
Roland TB-303 Bass Sequencer
Casio RZ-1
Korg Rhythm 55B
Alesis HR-16
Boss Dr. Rhythm DR-55
Ensoniq ASR-10
Akai 950
Akai MPC2000
E-mu SP1200

"I use everything and anything. I'm a drum machine fanatic."

COMPUTER/SOFTWARE:
Mac clone
ProTools TDM
Motor Mix (automated mixing board)
Digital Performer
Logic
Opcode Mastertracks Pro

KEYBOARDS/INSTRUMENTS:
Roland Juno-106
Roland D50
E-mu Proteus
E-mu Keys emulator
Casio SK-1
Casio SK-5
Fender Talent electric guitar

"I play almost every instrument, poorly. I've played guitar on a few of my records—Barman [It's Very Stimulating EP] and Prince Among Thieves, for example."

RECORDING/STUDIO:
CAD VX2PS Tube microphone
CAD E200 Condenser microphone
Avalon M5 microphone pre-amplifier

"I bring the same mic and same mic pre when I record at different studios in order to get consistent sound."

TC Electronics Finalizer
888 ADAT
882 ADAT
Mackie 32•8 mixing board
Yamaha NS-10 monitors
Radio Shack subwoofer
Alesis Point 7 monitor
Alesis Monitor 2

DJ:
Fisher ER 8020 8-track recorder
Gemini DS-1224 DJ sampler
Vestax 05 Pro mixer
Technics SL-1210 turntables
Univox Echo Chamber EC 80A

equipment photos courtesy of Prince Paul

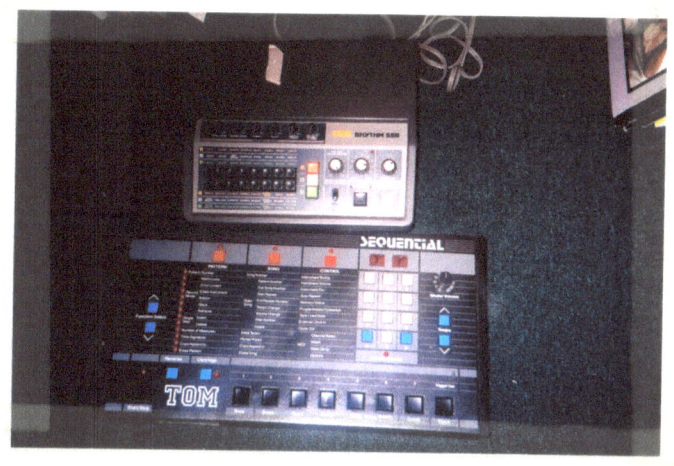

tablist

the world's first and only magazine dedicated to the art of turntablism

no.1 spring .002

x-ecutioners
mix master mike
swamp
mista sinista
scratch tips with:
skratchy and spaghetti seal

Don't be mad if you feel we dissed you, we probably did! Although, there are many people and publications we still have love for and they know that. Remember, Tablist Magazine is literally run by the same people it caters to. We are turntablists, producers, graphic designers, MC's and general population-type motherfuckers who are just into good shit. We represent the people who are used to getting the side story, the quarter of a page, uninformative blip. We can't help but be brutally honest. We are you.

To those who currently live in our world of turntablism, this is your newspaper. It will provide in-depth information and shed light on events and people you might not hear about in other publications. To the uneducated, the uninformed, and the unintroduced, this is your bible. Learn it. Live it.

For more info go to the-allies.com

Distribution ——————————————— Newsstands and Direct sales contact Counterflow Distribution (305)556-6326
Advertising Representatives ————————————— Christy Z. Pabon, Matt Hanrahan, and Kano (305)467-7128

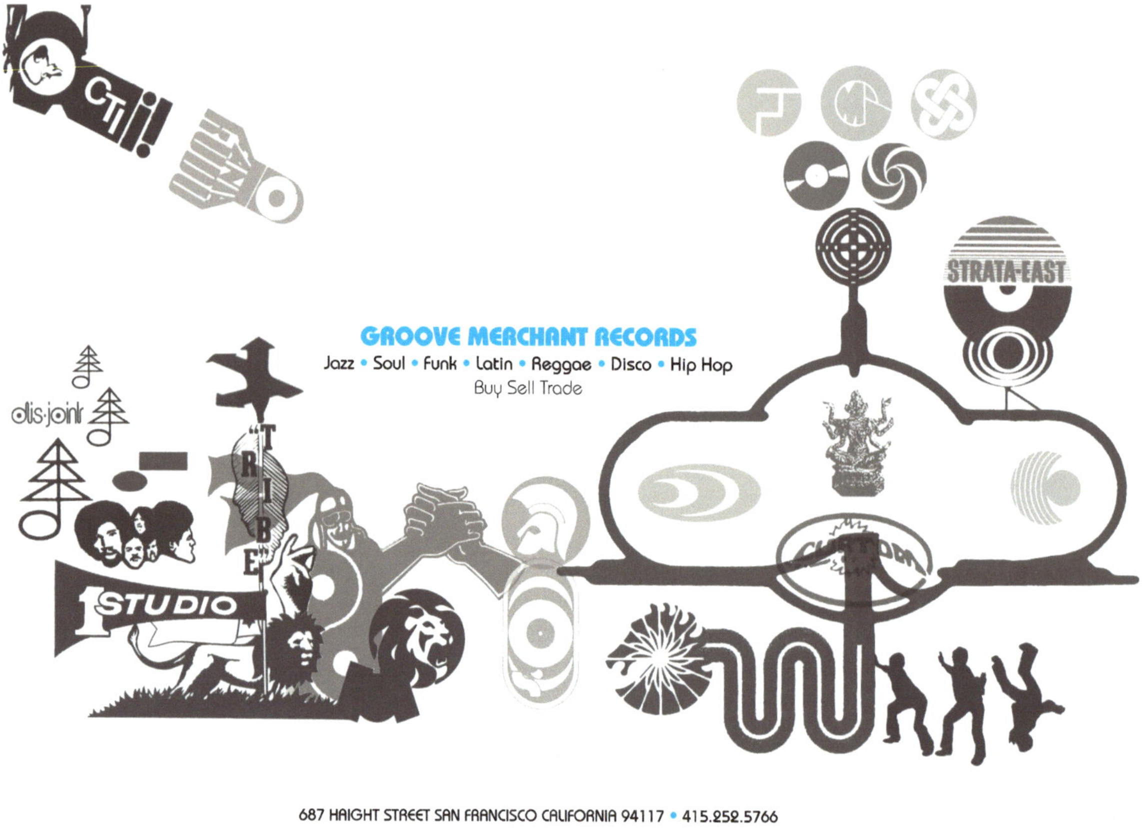

GROOVE MERCHANT RECORDS
Jazz • Soul • Funk • Latin • Reggae • Disco • Hip Hop
Buy Sell Trade

687 HAIGHT STREET SAN FRANCISCO CALIFORNIA 94117 • 415.252.5766

ADVENTURES IN THE COUNTERCULTURE
FROM HIP HOP TO HIGH TIMES
BY STEVEN HAGER
presented by **HIGH TIMES**

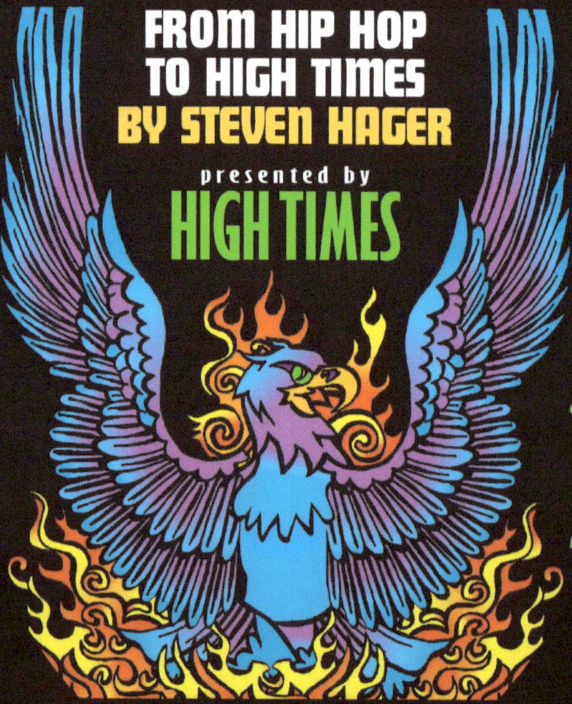

Steven Hager has been covering the counterculture for over 35 years. He founded *The Tin Whistle*, his first underground newspaper, in 1968, while still a high school student in Illinois. Twelve years later, he was the first reporter to travel to the South Bronx to document the history of hip hop. Hager became editor of *High Times* in 1988, founded the Cannabis Cup (the world's most prestigious marijuana festival) and became a leading figure in the hemp legalization movement of the '90s. For the first time, his most important writings have been collected into one volume.

"The best and most reliable history of the break-rap-graffiti subculture."
Robert Palmer

"The best article on the [JFK] assassination..."
Judge Jim Garrison

"Hager makes it a thrilling, intricate story..."
Greil Marcus

"The most historically accurate book on the subject..."
Mark Weinstein

"The outrageous energy of the participants...will carry the reader through this pop history."
Publishers Weekly

"Intelligent and extremely well-written..."
Dave Marsh

TO ORDER CALL 800-851-7039 OR GO TO HIGHTIMES.COM

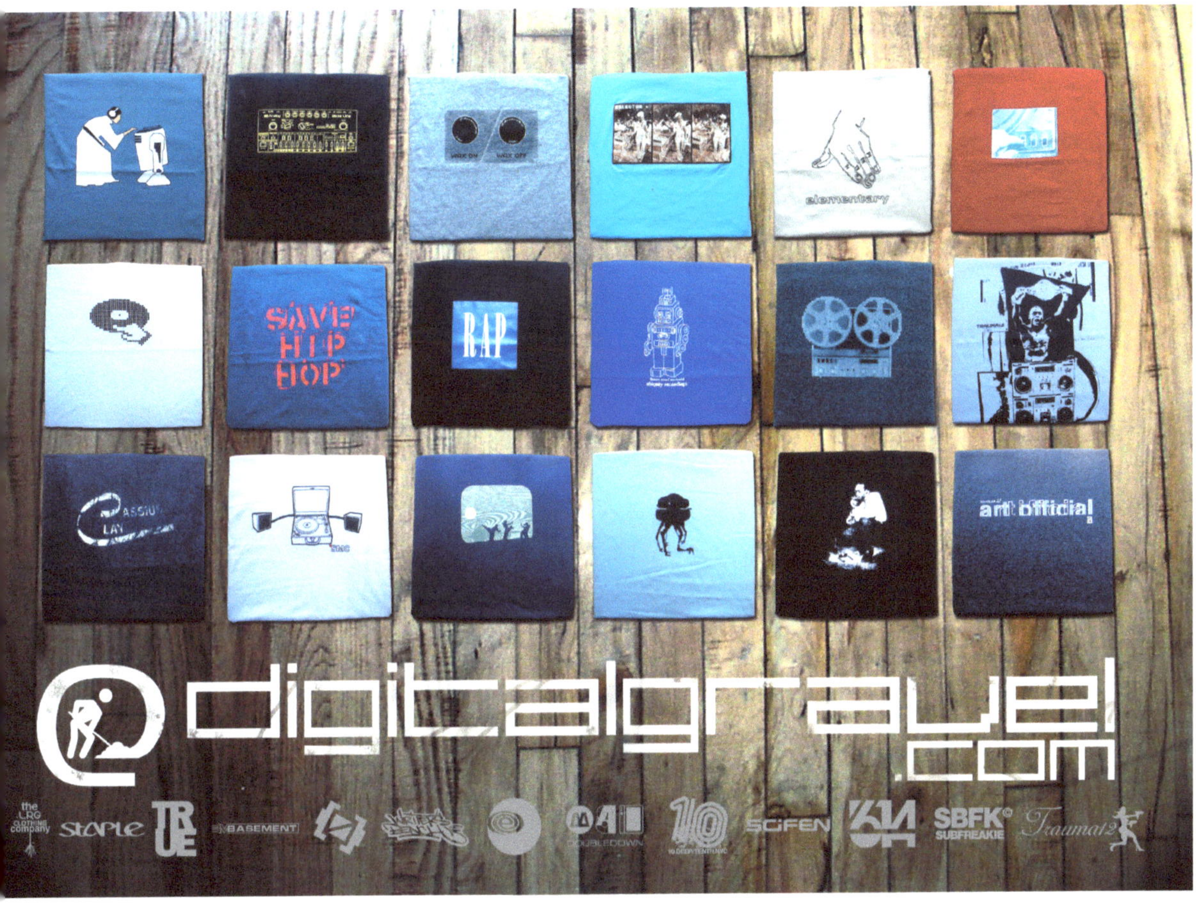

digitalgravel.com

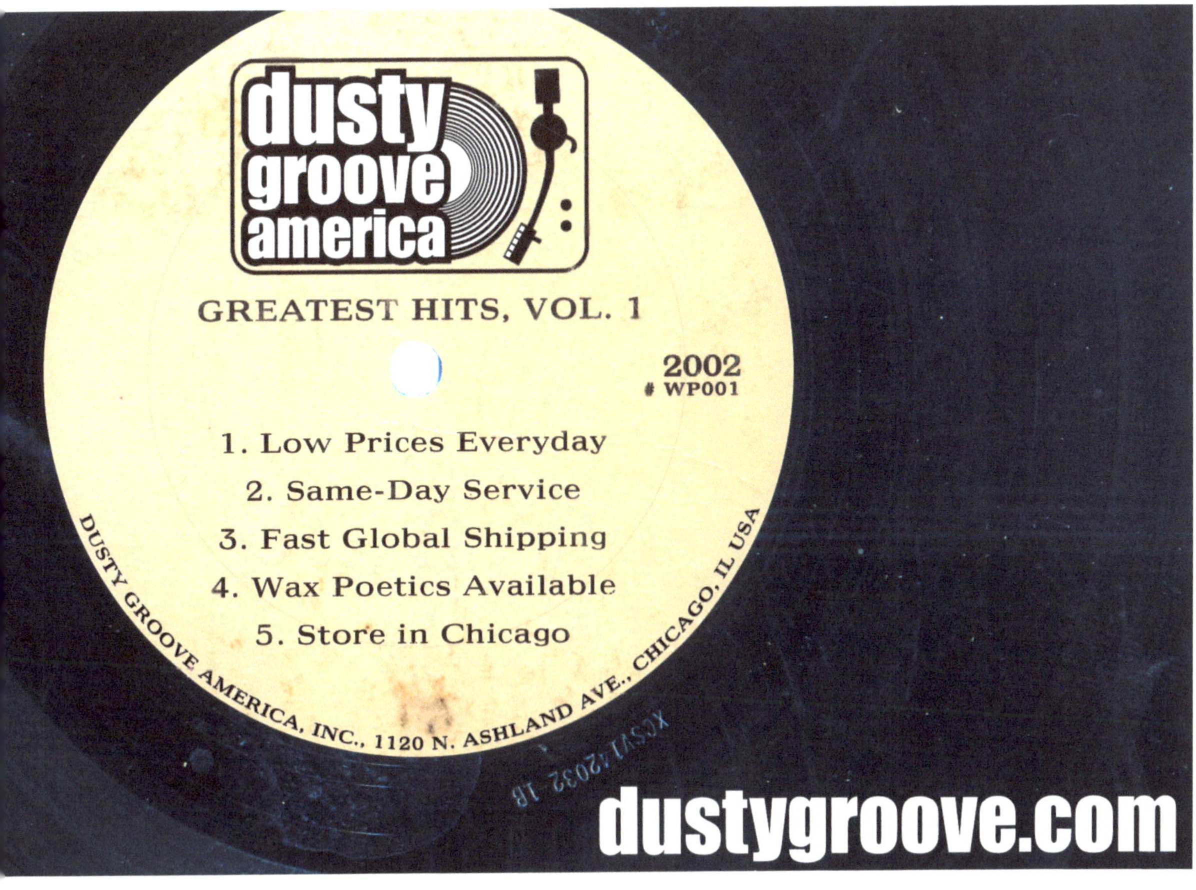

dusty groove america

GREATEST HITS, VOL. 1

2002
 # WP001

1. Low Prices Everyday
2. Same-Day Service
3. Fast Global Shipping
4. Wax Poetics Available
5. Store in Chicago

DUSTY GROOVE AMERICA, INC., 1120 N. ASHLAND AVE., CHICAGO, IL USA

dustygroove.com

waxpoetics.com

TIMOTHY McNEALY
and the
SAGITTARIUS BLACK BAND

May 15, 1972
Live at *Soul City* • Greenville Avenue

Hear audio portions of our
Timothy McNealy interview at
waxpoetics.com:

user name: shawn
password: audioshawn

out now: express rising "somebody's birthday" 45
due out: "chains and black exhaust" cd | express rising "jeux de ficelle" lp

1519 union ave. box 196 memphis tn 38104 | memphix-records.com

The Sound Library

We Buy and Sell Used Vinyl
Specializing in : Hip-Hop, Soul, Jazz, Funk, Soundtracks, Latin, Brazilian, Disco, R&B, and of course Sound Libraries

214 Avenue A (Between 13th & 14th Streets)
New York, NY 10009 USA
Tel : 212.598.9302
Fax : 212.598.9367
Email : thesoundlibrary@mac.com

photo by simon greenberg

Website (coming soon) : www.soundlibraryrecords.com

TSL THE SOUND LIBRARY

The Dynamic Funk Soul Excitement you've been waiting for has finally arrived.

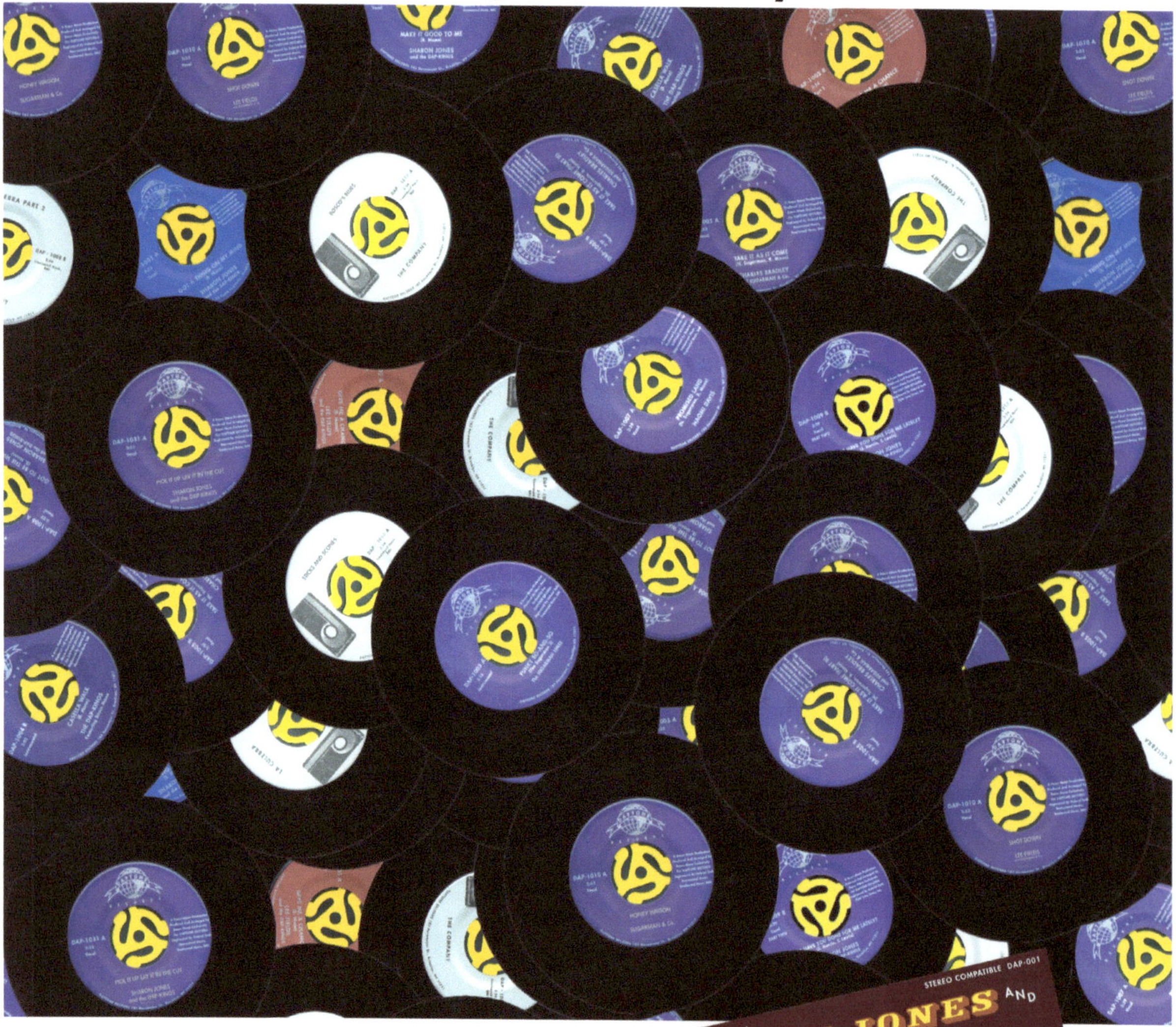

SHARON JONES AND THE DAP-KINGS

Full Length Album.
May 14th, 1972.

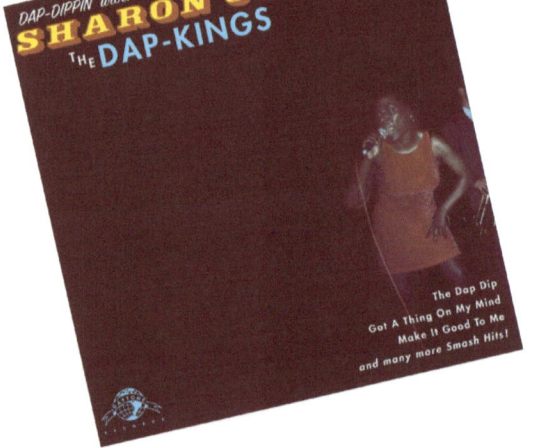

Your first source for Funk & Soul 45's.
www.daptonerecords.com

Dirty Finger B-Boys: Truly OdD, J.Rocc

mixwellusa.com

www.ingramcontent.com/pod-product-compliance
Lightning Source LLC
Chambersburg PA
CBHW040356190426
43201CB00039B/37